Moody

Evangelists

David Bennett

Marshall Pickering

Marshall Morgan and Scott
Marshall Pickering
34 – 42 Cleveland Street, London, W1P 5FB, U.K.

First published in 1989 by Marshall Morgan and Scott Publications Ltd
Part of the Marshall Pickering Holdings Group

British Library CIP Data

Bennett, David
  Moody and Sankey
  I. Title   II. Series
  266′.0092′2

  ISBN 0-551-01880-1

Text set in Baskerville by Avocet Robinson, Buckingham
Printed and bound in Great Britain by
Courier International Ltd, Tiptree, Essex

Other titles in Heroes of the Cross series

To be published shortly:

Dedication

For my wife Claire, and my children Keith and Lynne.

Acknowledgment

I would like to express my thanks to the following for their help in a variety of ways, from typing the manuscript to acquiring and providing material for this book: Eunice Brooks, Lynieve Neilen, Judy Newby, Judee Olechno, Cheryl Tough, Walter Osborn of the Moody Bible Institute Library, and the staff of the Chicago Historical Society.

David Bennett

Chapter 1

The sound of metal on stone rang loudly and clearly on the fine spring morning in Northfield, Massachusetts. Ed Moody chiselled methodically and energetically at the giant blocks of stone. Beads of sweat were visible on his brow. The veins stood out on his strong arms.

Suddenly, he stopped. His tools dropped to the ground and his hands went to his chest. His breathing, normally smooth and purposeful, now came in gasps. The pain was excruciating. He reached out to steady himself and slowly moved to a nearby chair.

He sat for what seemed an age, and gradually the pain declined. Moody was not a man to quit easily, but he knew that to try to go back to work would be foolish. He bent to pick up his tools, but an ache in both his arms made him decide to leave them where they were. He then made his way slowly home, along the wide, tree-lined street.

'You're home early, Ed,' said Betsey Moody. 'Lunch isn't ready yet.' Moody just stood in the doorway and said nothing. 'Ed, are you okay?' For the first time she really looked at him, and moved towards him as she saw his pallid face.

'It's a pain in the chest, Betsey,' he panted. 'Not as bad as it was, but I thought I'd better go to bed.'

Betsey, eight months pregnant, tried to help him in the direction of the lower floor bedroom, but he shrugged her off. 'It should be me supporting you, not the other way round.'

She followed him to the bedroom and helped him onto the bed. 'I'll go and get the doctor; you just rest.' Ed Moody said nothing.

Betsey left the room. She checked the baby upstairs, grabbed her shawl, and returned to the bedroom prior to her trip for the medic. Ed Moody was kneeling by the bedside, still and silent.

'Ed, are you okay? Ed?' She rushed towards her husband, but Edwin Moody had said his last prayer.

Edwin Moody and Betsey Holton had married on 3rd January, 1828. At the time of Edwin's death they had seven children. A month later Betsey gave birth to twins, a boy and a girl.

The sixth child of this union was Dwight Lyman Moody, a boy just over four years of age at the time of this tragedy. This, not surprisingly, was his earliest memory.

From then on life was a great struggle for Betsey Moody and her young family. Dedicated and stubborn, she refused to part with any of her children and worked tirelessly to provide for them. The two older boys soon began work and Dwight, while still quite young, helped a neighbouring farmer with his cows during the summer holidays.

Dwight Moody was no scholar, but he was gifted with a mischievous sense of fun and a natural boldness. Though these did not hide the limitations of his education, they did at times, seem to make people forget it.

On one occasion each child in Moody's class had to choose a poem or passage from literature and recite it to the assembled parents and dignitaries on speech night. Dwight chose the famous speech of Mark Antony from Shakespeare's *Julius Caesar*. To recite it was not enough, the young player had to perform it.

' "Friends, Romans, Countrymen," ' he began, ' "lend me your ears. I come to bury Caesar," ' he said, flourishing a hand in the direction of a large box brought along to serve as a coffin, ' "not to praise him." ' On went the monologue towards its climax.

' "And men have lost their reason. Bear with me; My heart is in the coffin there with Caesar . . ." '

So saying, Dwight solemnly reached over and slowly

lifted the lid of the 'coffin'. He reached in and the audience was shaken by a piercing howl from within. A large cat darted from its prison, ran past the assembled gathering and escaped from the hall. Dwight smiling broadly, concluded " 'And I must pause till it come back to me' ", then bowed. The crowd, momentarily shocked by the unexpected feline appearance, erupted into laughter and applause. Betsey Moody was not amused. Dwight L. Moody was not the easiest of her sons to raise.

The Moody family attended the nearby Unitarian Church, and the Sabbath was strictly observed, running from Saturday sundown until Sunday evening. The children, like it or not, attended the little church every Sunday. And though the boys protested, Betsey Moody would heed none of their objections. Daily Bible readings were another feature in the family, a fact remembered by Dwight throughout his life. Though the doctrine taught was different in some respects from that which Moody was to embrace later (the Unitarians deny the Trinity), the ethical teachings of the Scriptures were firmly and persistently taught to the growing children.

Four or five years after his father's death Dwight went to stay for a while with an older brother who had gone to work in Greenfield, a nearby town. The younger boy acquired part-time work milking cows for an elderly couple, and continued his schooling. Many years later Dwight reflected, 'I looked at the old man and saw he was cross. I took a good look at his wife, and thought she was crosser than the old man.' The youngster became very homesick.

He tried to persude his brother to take him back to Northfield, whose undulating pastures had suddenly become especially green and precious in his mind. While they were out walking and talking George Moody saw the figure of an elderly man approaching them. He recognised him instantly.

'Say, Dwight, see that man coming towards us?' he said.

The younger Moody peered through tear-reddened eyes and just nodded.

'He will give you a cent, Dwight. He always does with new boys in town,' said the older boy.

As the old man shuffled towards them, Dwight Moody watched him expectantly. When the man was close enough to be seen clearly, the boy became entranced by his face, which had a radiance unlike anything he had seen before. When he reached the boys he stopped, smiled and having removed Dwight's cap, placed his gnarled hand upon the boy's head. 'This is a new boy in town, isn't it?' he asked George.

'Yes, sir, he is. He's my brother just arrived from Northfield. His name's Dwight, sir.' The man replaced the cap.

Dwight was silently awaiting the expected gift, but the man had other things on his mind. 'Do you know, young Dwight, that there is a God in heaven that loves you?' He did not seem to expect an answer, and the boy, captivated by the stranger's enthusiasm, certainly had no intention of giving one. 'He loves you so much, my boy, that he sent his son, Jesus, to die for you. The good book tells us that "God so loved the world that he gave his only begotten Son, that whosoever believeth in him should not perish, but have everlasting life." God the Father sent his Son into this world because he loves you.' The old man's passionate voice and Christlikeness had made Dwight forget the desired cent coin, and he listened spellbound. He understood the man's words, yet in a strange way was mystified as to their meaning.

'He was nailed to the cross by wicked men, Dwight. He died for your sins, my boy. Isn't the Father's love great that he should send his "only begotten Son" into this world to die for you?' Again the younger Moody refrained from answering. It didn't even occur to him that an answer was expected.

'I have a gift for you, Dwight. Not a gift as great as that wonderful one God has given us, but I hope it will remind you of that gift, Jesus.' As he spoke he fished in his pocket and pulled out a shiny coin and gave it to the astonished boy.

8

Dwight stood speechless. After a momentary hesitation George nudged his younger brother. Suddenly, the boy remembered both his manners and his tongue. 'Oh, thank you, sir. Thank you very much.'

The man smiled and slowly walked away from them as the two boys stood in awed silence watching his departure. Dwight's homesickness was temporarily forgotten.

Chapter 2

As he grew through his teens Dwight became restless and tired of farm life. But his mother's insistence on his finishing school and the family's need of him on the farm kept him at Northfield. By the time his schooldays ended he had grown into a strapping young man of medium height, with a burning ambition to succeed. Farming wasn't for him. The big city lights beckoned. He, D.L. Moody, must leave home and go and make his fortune.

In the Spring of 1854, the seventeen-year-old farmer left home. He went first to Clinton, where one of his brothers worked, but quickly moved on to the larger more prosperous Boston.

In Boston two of his uncles, Samuel Socrates (known as S.S.) and Lemuel Holton, ran two shoe shops. He found his way to Uncle Samuel's shop in Court Street and saw him behind the counter. 'Hi, Uncle S.S.,' he greeted.

Samuel Holton's mouth fell open. He had visited his sister Betsey six months previously and learned that Dwight had ambitions about making a fortune in Boston. He knew that Dwight's abrupt appearance on the scene was not a social call. This uncouth country boy wanted a job in his shoe shop.

'Dwight Moody, what are you doing here?' he blurted out.

'D.L., Uncle S.S., D.L. Everyone calls me "D.L." now. I told yer I was goin' to come to Boston to make my fortune, so here I am.' Dwight hadn't bothered to remove his cap.

The older man was not impressed. How could he inflict this loudmouthed boy on his well-to-do customers? There was no way he would employ Dwight Moody, nephew or not.

'Well, I'm sorry, Dwight, but I haven't got time to talk to you. There are customers to serve.' And he brushed past the astonished boy and attended to a smartly dressed lady.

Dwight stood there for a while, and gradually it dawned on him that Uncle S.S. had no intention of giving him any more of his time. With a shrug of his broad shoulders he left the store and slowly walked in the direction of the other shop to see Uncle Lemuel, the junior partner.

The younger of the two uncles was more sympathetic, and invited D.L. to board with him while he searched for work. The hunt for employment was hard and discouraging. His brash manner and uneducated style of speech made him unacceptable to the employers he approached. After several days of fruitless job-hunting Dwight told Uncle Lemuel that he intended to go to New York.

'New York, D.L.? New York?' And how are you going to get there? You keep telling me you don't have any money.'

'I'll walk if I have to,' replied the despondent youth.

'Walk! Do you know how far New York is, boy?' responded Uncle Lemuel.

'I'm strong. I can do it.' He spoke boldly, but his feelings scarcely matched his outward bravado.

'Did you actually ask S.S. for a job when you saw him the other day?' questioned his uncle.

'Not exactly. But he knows I want one, and I'm not goin' beggin',' D.L. retorted.

'D.L., put your pride in your pocket and go to S.S. and ask him outright for a position.'

'I'll not do it, Uncle. I'm not goin' beggin'.' With that the defiant young man turned on his heels, and stormed out of the house.

The next day Dwight had reconsidered, and slowly wended his way to Uncle Samuel's shop. 'Uncle, I need a job. Would you give me a chance? I promise to do whatever you want,' begged the boy, feeling miserable and humiliated.

'Now listen here, Dwight Moody,' began S.S. 'If you want to come to work here and do the best you can, and do it right, I'll give you an opportunity. Mark you, I insist on a few things. When you don't know how to do something, you'll ask. I expect you to go to church and Sunday School every Sunday. You mustn't attend any place that your mother wouldn't approve of. Now, if you'll accept those conditions, I'll employ you. You can have till tomorrow to think it over.'

'I don't need that long, Uncle,' said D.L. softly. 'I promise now. When do I start?' For the first time in days Dwight Moody smiled.

D.L. was true to his word. On Sunday he dutifully went to Mount Vernon Congregational Church and Sunday School, not willingly, but as 'part of the deal'. The Sunday School superintendent was perplexed. What could he do with this new scholar? It was clear that the boy was uneducated, and he sensed an air of mischievousness which could prove disruptive. With a stroke of inspiration, which could only have come from God, Julius Palmer decided to place him in Ed Kimball's class.

D.L. was taken to the appropriate room. The class had already begun.

'We have a new boy for you, Mr Kimball,' said Palmer. 'His name's Dwight Moody, but he likes to be called "D.L." '

Kimball was younger than the boy expected; about thirty he guessed. As the teacher rose to greet him, Moody saw that he was unusually tall.

'You're very welcome! D.L., is that right?' asked Kimball.

Moody nodded. The other boys in the class eyed the newcomer with curiosity.

'Sit down over here near me.' Ed Kimball directed his

new charge to a vacant chair. 'Here's a Bible, D.L. We are studying John chapter 10.'

D.L. took the Bible and sat down. He thought for a moment, and found himself wishing that he had paid more attention when his mother had read the Bible at home. 'Where is John?' he asked himself, and began thumbing through Genesis in a vain attempt to find the gospel.

The whole class noticed. The boys gave each other knowing smiles, but the teacher came to the rescue, giving Moody his own opened Bible and taking the one D.L. was leafing through. A quick, stern glance round the class made it clear that Ed Kimball would not tolerate the new scholar being victimised.

Moody was impressed, not by the lesson, but by his teacher's act of kindness. He vowed to himself that he would 'stick by the fellow who had stood by him and had done him a turn like that'.

Dwight was quickly becoming successful in his new-found vocation. He discovered that he enjoyed selling shoes, and he was very good at it.

Uncle Samuel had mixed feelings. Sales were up, and he knew that his nephew was the main reason for that. But the boy's speech was so uncouth. Boston people, after all, were educated and refined. He winced as he listened to the boy's tortured grammar and slick salesmanship. But results were results, and he was a businessman after all.

One morning D.L. received an unexpected visitor at work, Ed Kimball. Kimball did not believe that a Sunday School teacher's responsibilities for his class ended at the conclusion of school on Sunday. He was concerned about his charges, and this rough-and-ready but likeable boy had wormed his way into his heart. He had decided to challenge Dwight Moody with the claims of Jesus Christ, and though he was hesitant about doing so while the boy was at work, he felt convinced that the time was ripe.

He found Dwight in the room behind the shop wrapping up shoes.

D.L. looked up as the tall figure entered the room, 'Hi,

Mr Kimball. What are yer doin' here?'

Kimball placed his hand upon the boy's shoulder and, doing his best to look casual, placed his right foot on a shoe-box. 'D.L., there's something I want to tell you.' The words came out slowly.

Moody sensed a certain tenderness, but said nothing.

'D.L., I believe that the Lord Jesus Christ loves you. Do you remember the first time you came to my class? We learned about Jesus as the Good Shepherd. D.L., all of us have sinned. Isaiah says, "All we like sheep have gone astray, we have turned every one to his own way." You see, D.L., I'm a sinner, you're a sinner. But the beautiful thing is that "the Lord hath laid on him the iniquity of us all". When Jesus died on the cross, he bore your sins, D.L. He did that because he loved you.'

D.L. felt uncomfortable, yet at the same time fascinated. He noticed that tears were welling up in Ed Kimball's eyes as he proceeded to tell him about his need of salvation.

Before the Sunday School teacher left that room behind Samuel Holton's shoe store that day, Dwight Lyman Moody was born again.

Dwight Moody had become 'a new creature', and he found himself with a new love for God's creation.

George Wade Robinson was to write later:

> *Heaven above is softer blue,*
> *Earth around is sweeter green;*
> *Something lives in every hue,*
> *Christless eyes have never seen.*

Though Moody was no poet, he knew the experience. The world seemed a different place, and he was a new man. He later reflected, 'I had not a bitter feeling against any man, and I was ready to take all men to my heart.'

He was never one to sit and let things happen, and he soon applied for membership at his church. Mount Vernon had a rigorous method of interviewing prospective members, and on this occasion Moody had bitten off more than he could chew.

He was invited to present himself before the interviewing committee, comprising several deacons and Ed Kimball. D.L. entered the room boldly enough, but when he saw the assembled church leaders, he became unusually nervous. Even the presence of his kindly Sunday School teacher failed to calm him.

The deacons were not unsympathetic, but the young convert was out of his depth.

'Have you been converted, Mr Moody?' asked one of them.

Dwight hesitated. 'Er, yes.'

'Are you a sinner?' asked another.

Another pause. 'I guess.'

'Do you trust Christ alone for salvation?'

He certainly knew the answer to that. 'Yes.'

The questions continued. 'Yes', 'No', 'I think so' answered the candidate. No eloquence, but he had survived it so far. Then one of the deacons asked, 'Mr Moody, what has Christ done for us all – for you – which entitles him to our love?'

D.L.'s mind was in a whirl. What was the answer to that? 'I'm not sure I know,' he said hesitantly. 'I think Christ has done a great deal for us. But I don't think of anything particular as I know of.' As he glanced at the embarrassed looks on the faces of the interviewers, D.L. knew he had failed.

But D.L. Moody was not easily denied. Though his knowledge of doctrine was limited, his faith was real. Next time he applied he was accepted.

Though life was going well for him, D.L. felt he needed a change. Boston was so stuffy. He knew people at the church frowned on his frequent comments at the church prayer meetings, and though his relationship with S.S. was outwardly friendly, he sensed that his uncle would be happier if his nephew worked for someone else. So in

September 1856, nineteen years old, Dwight left Boston and travelled west to Chicago.

'I went into a prayer meeting last night,' wrote Moody to his mother soon after his arrival there, 'and as soon as I made myself known I had friends enough. After meeting they came to me, and seemed to be glad to see me as if I were their earthly brother. God is the same here as he was in Boston, and in him I can find peace.'

D.L. found Chicago to his liking. He loved its busyness and the dynamic feeling of growth, yet he was shocked by the desecration of the Sabbath. In another letter home he wrote, 'It is so wicked the stores are open on the Sabbath, a great many of them.'

He found a position in a shoe shop run by Charles Wiswall who quickly came to appreciate his new employee's selling skills. Very few customers who entered the shop left without a purchase, and when things were quiet D.L. went outside and persuaded passers-by to 'come and see the new range of shoes'. His powers of persuasion and amiability combined to make him a highly successful salesman.

He became a member of Plymouth Congregational Church, and the enthusiasm and technique he used in his employment he also utilised in Christ's service. He rented four pews in the church and regularly filled them with colleagues from work, staff from other nearby shops, and people just out for a Sunday stroll.

Although Chicago people were much less snobbish than those in Boston, D.L. still found himself in trouble when he spoke or prayed at prayer meetings. His bluntness and peculiar phrasing caused the members at Plymouth to request that he keep silent until he had learned better.

Though he did not become disloyal to his own church, his enthusiasm to serve found him attending services and helping in Methodist, Baptists and Presbyterian churches as well. His energy was boundless and he thought little of denominational barriers. One Sunday afternoon Moody came across a small Sunday School in Wells Street, and offered his services.

'We don't need teachers, young man,' responded the superintendent. 'We already have twelve and we only have sixteen scholars.'

'You sound like the kinda school I can help, mister,' said D.L. This suited him down to the ground. He did not feel able to teach, but he had become an expert at 'drumming up Sunday School scholars'. Moody vanished and did not reappear that day. During the week the superintendent forgot the visit from the young country boy. The next Sunday he was given a sharp reminder when D.L. turned up in time for Sunday School with eighteen dishevelled boys.

'I've got you some new boys, mister,' he said with a grin. 'Not very many, I'm afraid, but they've all got souls to save.'

The man's mouth fell open, but he quickly recovered and ushered his new charges into the mission. Moody followed and sat through the session. Each week he continued his efforts and the Sunday School grew larger and larger.

One Sunday he noticed a new teacher, a teenage girl, whom he had previously seen in the First Baptist Church. During the afternoon he found his eyes wandering in her direction, and not infrequently he noticed that she was looking at him. Though Emma Revell was clearly from a more sophisticated background than he (she was the daughter of a shipbuilder, Fleming H. Revell), he did not hesitate to go up to her and introduce himself after school. D.L. found the shy fifteen-year-old captivating. Surprisingly, she was as taken by this rough-and-ready salesman as he was by her.

Emma had been born in England and had emigrated to America with her family when she was six. Quiet and cultured, but with a love of fun, she seemed the perfect foil for D.L.

Chapter 3

In 1858 Moody established a new Sunday School in a saloon near the North Side Market. He was in his element. His new mission school catered for the worst slum area in Chicago, The Sands, where every type of crime and moral degradation could be found. Dwight's genius at 'dragging them in' came to the fore again. Attendances at the school quickly increased.

He gathered around him a loyal band of workers, including a young architect named J.B. Stillson and a young businessman, John Carter. Moody and Stillson had known each other for some time, having frequently joined in evangelistic labours around the bars and on board the ships moored in the river.

The methods employed were unusual. Moody and his co-workers realised from the beginning that a lengthy lesson would not work. Instead the sessions were centred around a lot of singing led by Carter, punctuated by brief Bible stories, and with opportunities for the children to let off steam.

It wasn't long before the Sunday School began to outgrow its premises. But with the approval of the Mayor they were permitted to use a hall above the market. On Saturday nights it was used for dancing, so each Sunday morning they had to clear up the mess and prepare for their scholars.

Early each Sunday afternoon D.L. would tour the slums. 'Come on, boys,' he called, 'come along to Sunday School. What d'yer mean pullin' a face like that? Not even yer mother would love yer lookin' like that.' The boys laughed. The rough edges which had so irritated the well-to-do

Bostonians, and even many Christians in Chicago, helped him reach children who knew little or nothing of English grammar or the God who loved them.

'Let me see what I have here,' said Moody laughing, fishing in his pocket and pulling out some sweets. The boys goggled at the tempting items. 'Of course, no Sunday School, no sweets,' said the evangelist putting the sweets back in his pocket, and turning to walk off. After a few steps he stopped and turned his head. Sure enough the boys were following him.

'Do you have brothers and sisters too?' enquired Moody.

'Yes,' came the chorus.

'Well, s'pect they like sweets too, so yer better go and get 'em. I'll wait.'

Off rushed the boys returning with the other children. Moody, like the pied piper, led the way, the troop of dirty children following close behind.

The school continued to grow but finance was an acute problem. They had no seats at all; the children either stood or sat on the hard floor. But Moody was determined to remedy the situation, so, after discussion with his helpers, he decided to approach Christian businessmen and ask for their support.

One such was John V. Farwell, a businessman he had met at a Methodist church. Farwell typified the American dream. He had risen from poverty to riches, though still only in his thirties, and owned Chicago's main store. He agreed to help, and Moody invited him to the Sunday School the next Sunday afternoon.

John Farwell accepted the invitation. As he approached the hall the din emanating from it seemed to grow louder and louder. He walked through the door and was astonished to see hundreds of poorly dressed children chasing each other around the hall and playing games. When some of the youngsters spotted their well dressed visitor, they rushed towards him. 'Clean yer shoes for yer, mister,' several called. The lanky visitor looked down at the boys at his feet, fighting for the privilege of cleaning his already sparkling shoes.

'Is Mr Moody here yet?' he asked.

'Yeh, mister. He's over there,' said one, pointing across the hall to the platform.

Farwell looked and saw the stocky bearded figure of Moody. He walked towards him, dodging the excited children as he went. Moody spotted him and came to meet him. 'I'm glad yer came, John,' he said with a grin, slapping his friend on the shoulder. 'Quite a handful, eh?'

'Yes, D.L., quite a handful.'

'I'll get 'em to stop the noise and you can speak to 'em. Not too long now.' Moody stood on a box and with a stentorian shout brought the gathering to a reasonable imitation of silence. 'Children, we have a very special guest here today, Mr J.V. Farwell. He is going to speak to us.'

Moody stepped down, and the astonished visitor did his best to say something worthwhile to an audience, the nature of which he could never have imagined existed before that day.

As Farwell concluded, Moody came to the fore again. 'Children,' he called, 'I have some news for yer. Mr Farwell is to be our new Superintendent. Let's give him a cheer.'

The children obliged lustily.

John Farwell was taken aback. Moody hadn't mentioned that. The idea had no immediate appeal to him. But he could see the importance of this work, and gradually he became sympathetic to the doubtful privilege. Anyway, he thought, how can I back out now? So Superintendent of the North Market Mission Sunday School he became.

After a brief involvement in the work, and a close observation of the dynamic Moody's methods, he decided to lighten his friend's burdens. He bought him a horse. From then, instead of trudging the streets persuading children to come to hear the gospel, Moody carried out the same task on horseback. Each time he returned to the hall a swarm of children accompanied him, some on the horse, most following behind.

D.L. also became involved with the Young Men's Christian Association, for which he worked with his usual enthusiasm. He was involved in organising the daily noon prayer meeting. At first it was poorly attended, but gradually it blossomed into a vital ministry.

He continued his Sunday School work with his usual vigour. But his obsession seemed to be more with numbers than with souls. Children by the hundreds he brought to the school, but his vision hardly included the individual.

Then in June 1860 he received a visit at work from one of the Sunday School teachers. This teacher had never looked particularly robust, and his health had been deteriorating for some months, but Moody was shocked by his appearance that day. He was pale and drawn, with a cough that continually racked his thin body.

'Sit down, Ben. Do sit down,' fussed Moody. 'You sound as though you should be in bed, not here. What's the trouble?

'My lungs have been haemorrhaging . . .' He broke off in another fit of coughing. He put a handkerchief to his mouth, then continued. 'The doctor tells me I won't survive another winter in Chicago. It's those winter winds that do it. I'm going back home, and even there the doctor doesn't expect me to live long. I suppose I'm going home to die.'

Moody felt a lump in his throat. 'But you're anxious on somethin' else, Ben. What is it?' he managed to say.

'My class, D.L. Those girls. None of them know Christ. Sometimes I think I have done them more harm than good,' he replied, then coughed again.

'I did your class once when you were away. They are not easy girls to deal with. They all need saving,' Moody said, then became unusually quiet. His companion sat silently too, with a troubled look on his face.

Suddenly D.L. burst out, 'Why don't we visit those girls? We can hire a carriage and you can tell each one of them how you feel.'

The teacher perked up. 'Yes, D.L. And you'll come with me?'

'Yes, of course.'

So they visited each of the girls. The teacher told each one about her need of the Saviour, and Moody prayed for her salvation.

Years later Moody recalled, 'I have never done such a thing as to pray God to convert a young lady, there and then. But we prayed, and God answered our prayer.'

One by one the girls in tears of repentance were born again, and the two soul-winners returned home with tears of joy.

Dwight called the class together for a prayer meeting that night, because the teacher was due to leave the following day. All of them came. And Moody was profoundly moved as one by one the girls prayed for their dying teacher.

The next evening D.L. went to the station to bid farewell to the sick man. As the two of them stood on the platform, one of the girls appeared, and then another, and another. Shortly the whole class, without prearrangement, was assembled. They tried to sing a hymn together but they all broke down. So Moody prayed before the train was boarded.

The last any of them saw of the teacher was him standing on the platform at the rear of the train, one finger pointing upwards, indicating where he would next meet his class.

Chapter 4

Dwight Moody had left Wiswall's employ at the end of 1857, and joined the company C.N. Henderson, another shoe firm. He and his new employer formed a close friendship, and he served as a travelling salesman and debt collector. After a short time Henderson died and Moody joined another organisation; Bul, Hill and Granger. Throughout all these changes the desire to become rich, which had been his driving force, gradually faded. Replacing it was his zeal for Jesus Christ.

In September 1860 he left his job and began to work full time for his Lord. 'I have decided to give God all my time,' he told his employers. He had saved up to prepare for his new lifestyle, but he knew that the money would not last forever, so he lived frugally. He slept in a room in the Methodist Church used by the YMCA, and ate sparingly.

Fleming Revell, his future father-in-law, estimated that in his last year of business Moody earned $5,000. In his first year in full-time Christian work his income was $150.

The dying Sunday School teacher had set him an example he would never forget. From now on D.L. Moody was not just concerned with numbers, he was concerned with souls.

The North Market Sunday School was not Moody's Sunday School, nor Farwell's Sunday School. They believed it belonged to the children it catered for. Consequently when the school became structured in classes, the children were given the unique privilege of selecting their own teacher. Any teachers who found themselves without a class quietly left the school.

'Butcher' Kilroy had earned his nickname. Many of the children in The Sands had found themselves victims of his anger and viciousness. Bigger than most of his age, 'Butcher' was feared by all. But North Market Mission said 'No' to no one. And when he was invited by a younger boy to attend, the audacity of the request left him with no option but to see what it was all about.

Kilroy lived up to his reputation and over the following weeks went from class to class, disrupting each one. Nobody could control him. Kilroy seemed to enjoy reducing teachers and scholars to tears.

'We can't do anything with him, Mr Moody,' said a frustrated teacher who had had the misfortune of trying to teach the boy that day. 'We'll just have to stop him coming.'

'But we can't do that, brother,' stated D.L. firmly. 'The worse these children are, the more they need to come. The more they need Christ! We ain't gonna stop him coming. What do you say, John?' said Moody to his superintendent.

'You're right, of course, D.L. But though we've learned to live with not a few troublemakers, and seen some of them converted, he's the worst we've had,' replied Farwell. 'It's not easy I know, but we must keep trying. We must keep praying. That little lad that brought him in the first place, young Jacky, tells me he's praying for him. Can we do less?'

Jacky was no fairweather Christian. No one in The Sands could be. Every day he prayed for 'Butcher' Kilroy. Gradually the tough lad began to change. His behaviour became more controlled. He began to ask questions. Then, at the end of one Sunday School session in autumn, the young tearaway walked slowly up to D.L. He grabbed hold of the man's coat sleeve and, as Moody turned, the boy's thin lips broke into a rare smile. 'Mr Moody,' he blurted out, 'I b'lieve in Jesus.'

Moody's face lit up and he put his big hands on the boy's shoulder. 'So do I, my boy. So do I, more than ever now. God be praised!'

On Sunday, 25th November, 1860, the President-elect of the USA, Abraham Lincoln, visited Chicago. John Farwell, who had had a short involvement in politics, invited him to the Sunday School. He accepted on the condition that he would not be asked to address the school.

Lincoln was received enthusiastically by the children. He only stayed for a short time and as he was about to leave, Moody stood up and said, 'We thank Mr Lincoln for his visit today. He came on the condition that he be not asked to speak. But I am sure if he wishes to say somethin' we would all be happy to hear him.'

Lincoln looked at Moody in surprise, but like many before and after him saw no way of escape, so he spoke briefly to the children, urging them to practise what they were learning.

On 4th March the following year Lincoln was inaugurated as President. Six weeks later the American Civil War began.

In war, as in other things, Moody saw the issues in black and white, with no shades of grey. The northern states were the 'goodies' while the southern slave-holding states were the 'baddies'. But, as he was to demonstrate during the tragic four years of warfare, D.L. Moody was interested in bringing Confederate prisoners-of-war to Christ just as much as Yankee soldiers.

Under the auspices of the YMCA, Moody and Ben Jacobs, who ran another Sunday School, were invited to act as unofficial chaplains to the northern troops being trained at Camp Douglas, just south of Chicago. They knew well enough that it was the job of the soldier to fight and, if need be, to die for the flag he had enlisted under. Platitudes and words of comfort were no use to men who might die soon; they needed the Gospel. Moody and Jacobs made sure they heard it.

Moody's experience at public speaking, or even presenting the Gospel one to one, had been very limited. He was painfully aware of his lack of education and meagre

Bible knowledge, but the needs of men in war were so immediate that when he received the opportunity to speak for Christ, he knew he must take it. And many came to Christ before facing the horrors of such battles as Bull Run and Shiloh.

Early in 1862 he went to work among the troops in Tennessee, where General Grant had captured Fort Donelson for the north. Moody was shocked by what he saw. The dead lay where they had been shot with no one to bury them. The injured, in makeshift hospitals, moaned and screamed as they waited for treatment, or suffered amputations often without chloroform.

During one visit to a military hospital Moody was awakened from a brief sleep. 'Mr Moody, Mr Moody. One of the dying has asked to speak to you.' It was one of his helpers from the Christian Commission, which had been formed to minister to the soldiers. D.L. got up, grabbed his Bible and followed his colleague to the man's bedside.

As Moody approached, the soldier tried to sit up but failed. 'Chaplain,' he whispered hoarsely after Moody had knelt by his side, 'I'm scared to die. Can you help me?' His voice was desperate. His face was ashen.

Moody said nothing for a moment. He tried to bring his emotions under control. Then he muttered, 'I'd take you right up in my arms and carry you into the Kingdom of God if I could; but I can't do it. I can't help you die.'

'Who can, Chaplain? Who can? I'm scared!'

'The Lord Jesus can. That's why he came.'

A look of pain came over the man's face, and he shook his head. 'He can't save me. I've sinned all my life.'

'But he came to save sinners. Listen to the words of the Lord Jesus.' Moody leafed through his Bible and began to read from John chapter three. As Moody reached verses 14 and 15 the dying man became agitated. 'Is that really there, Chaplain?' he asked.

'Yes.'

'Read it again. Please read it again.'

'And as Moses lifted up the serpent in the wilderness,

even so must the Son of Man be lifted up: that whosoever believeth in him should not perish but have eternal life.'

'That's good, Chaplain. Please read it again.'

Moody obliged with a third reading.

When Moody looked up from the Bible the man's face had changed. Gone was the agitation; in its place was a smile. The man seemed weaker though, and in a barely audible whisper Moody heard the man repeating those precious verses. A few hours later he was dead. Like the thief on the cross he had found the Saviour at the eleventh hour.

After the battle of Shiloh in April that year, Moody and some associates from the Christian Commission accompanied the injured in a boat on the Tennessee River. It was apparent that many of the men would never make it to hospital, so the Christians determined to tell each one about Christ. 'We must not let a man die on this boat without telling him of Christ and heaven,' urged Moody.

As they gave water to the wounded, they told each one about the heavenly Father who loved him and the Christ who died for him.

That same year Camp Douglas was transformed into a camp for Confederate prisoners, and Moody applied for a permit to visit them. He and James Hawley found the prisoners very responsive, and held meetings for them twice a day. Many came to Christ.

Chapter 5

On 28th August, 1862, while the war raged on, Dwight Moody married Emma Revell. During the troubled first year of the war, with his efforts divided between his work for the soldiers, the Sunday School and the YMCA, Emma had become more and more his confidante. On the principal that opposites attract, the two found themselves head over heels in love. Yet their relationship was not one in which their love for each other excluded outsiders. As Dwight laboured for the causes God had placed on his heart, Emma encouraged and advised him. She put no brake on his efforts, even though he drove himself so hard.

Their financial situation was precarious as D.L. refused to accept any regular salary. Their first home was on the north side of the river in the poorer part of Chicago.

On New Year's Day, the Moodys were disturbed by a knock on the door. When Emma opened the door she came face to face with the beaming John Farwell. Parked outside was a carriage.

'Happy New Year, Emma,' wished the enthusiastic Farwell. 'You and D.L. get ready straight away. I'm taking you out.'

'Where to?' asked the astonished Emma.

'You'll see! You'll see! Just get ready.'

Farwell's excitement was contagious, and Dwight and Emma bubbled with expectation as the carriage took them to a street of newly built houses.

'Who lives here, John?' asked D.L.

'Be patient! You'll see!' replied his friend.

They got down from the carriage and, led by Farwell, approached one of the new buildings. He fished in his pocket, pulled out a key and opened the door. As they entered, they were greeted by dozens of friends and supporters, who welcomed them enthusiastically.

After a few minutes Farwell quietened the gathering and began a brief speech. 'We must keep you in suspense no longer. D.L. and Emma, with love and appreciation from many of your friends present here today, we would like you to accept this gift of the house in which you are standing, and all its furniture.

For a few moments D.L. stood in silent disbelief. Then he began to look around him, and his face lit up. Emma had beaten him to it. Her face was already beaming.

'All this for us?' were the first words the astonished Dwight could utter.

Farwell smiled. 'Yes, of course.'

D.L. could feel the tears in his eyes and the lump in his throat as he gasped, 'Thank you. Thank you so very much.'

The work at the North Market Mission had progressed well. It had been Moody's hope that the converts made through its ministry would be placed in suitable churches. Unfortunately none of the churches seemed 'suitable'. It gradually dawned on him that he needed to erect a building and found a church made up of the converts of the mission's activities.

Moody, by now considerably overweight, set about raising the necessary funds for the buildings. This task could not have been easy, because the war was still being fought. But the necessary $20,000 was acquired and the building erected. It was opened as the Illinois Street Church early in 1864. Though organised under Congregational auspices, it was never fully recognised as a Congregational church, and functioned as an independent evangelical church.

Though Moody was unquestionably the leader of it, he didn't preach. He still believed that such a role was beyond him. The pulpit was occupied mainly by students from the Congregational Theological Seminary. One Sunday evening no student appeared and John Farwell persuaded Moody to preach. From then on the students preached in the mornings and he in the evenings. Not that he found preparation of sermons easy, but he was driven on by a God-given desire to be what God wanted him to be.

His preaching was full of judgment. Emma felt he emphasised that aspect of the Word too much. In later years Moody criticised his early efforts: 'I preached that God hated sinners and that he was standing behind them with a double-edged sword, ready to cut off the heads of sinners.'

In the winter of 1866 – 67 Emma suffered so badly from asthma that the doctor advised a sea trip. Her husband had felt an increasing desire to travel to England. He longed to hear the great preacher Charles Haddon Spurgeon, and to meet George Muller, that great man of faith, and George Williams, the founder of the YMCA.

They left America for England on 24th February, 1867, and Moody discovered that he was prone to seasickness. Shortly after his arrival, D.L., at his most unprophetic, said, 'One trip across the water is enough for me. I don't expect to visit this country again.'

He sought out those it had been his desire to meet, but an encounter with a 'lesser light' had more long-term influence on him.

That significant meeting was with a short, baby-faced preacher from Lancashire, Harry Moorhouse. They met in Dublin, and Moorhouse volunteered to preach in the Illinois Street Church on his proposed trip to America. Moody had never heard of this man, dubbed the 'Boy Preacher', and there was nothing in him that led D.L. to feel enthusiastic about accepting the offer. He just suggested that Moorhouse contact him upon arrival in the USA, and then forgot the matter.

The Moodys returned to Chicago. Early in 1868 D.L. received a letter from Moorhouse, posted in New York, advising of his availability to preach. Moody was annoyed, but Emma wrote back on his behalf advising the Lancastrian, if he travelled to Chicago, to make sure that he looked them up. Nothing was mentioned about preaching. A second letter arrived from Moorhouse, and Moody replied in a similar vein to Emma's letter. A third letter arrived from the persistent Englishman giving his expected time of arrival. D.L. was trapped.

The following Thursday and Friday Moody was due to be away from his church, so it was agreed to use the visitor for the two weekday meetings. When D.L. returned he casually asked his wife, 'How did that Irishman go?' (Moody thought he was Irish because they had met in Dublin.) 'How do they like him?'

'They like him very much,' replied Emma.

Moody looked surprised and continued, 'Did you hear him?'

'Yes.'

'Did you like him?'

'Yes, very much. He preached twice on John 3:16. I think you will like him too, though he preaches differently from you.'

'Different! How's that?' sensing a significance in his wife's words.

'Well, he tells sinners God loves them.'

'Well, he's wrong, then,' stated Moody dogmatically.

'D.L., when you hear him you will agree with him, because he backs up everything he says with the Bible.'

Moody had a great respect for his wife's opinions and put forward no objection to Moorhouse preaching again. The 'Boy Preacher' preached every night for a further week, and the crowds came to hear him. Each occasion he preached from John 3:16. Each night he expounded the Word from Genesis to Revelation, detailing the love of God throughout Scripture. Every night his sermon was different.

This was a revelation to Dwight Moody on two counts. Firstly, he was enthralled by the visitor's thorough use of Scripture. Secondly, for the first time he realised that God loved not only Christians, but non-Christians too.

He spent a lot of time with Moorhouse during that week, and learned about his method of studying the Word. When Harry Moorhouse left Chicago, Moody began to immerse himself in Scripture in a completely new way.

31

Chapter 6

Dwight Moody was tone deaf. Yet the singing of great hymns by a great congregation moved him deeply. He recognised the importance of music in Christian worship, even though he himself could only benefit from it secondhand.

In the 1860s he had used a singer named Philip Phillips to aid him in his services. Philip Bliss, composer of the hymn 'Hold the fort for I am coming' (based on an incident in the now concluded Civil War), had helped him in the same way. But Phillips was rarely in Chicago, and Bliss had become choirmaster of another church, so he, too, was unavailable. Moody knew that he needed someone of the calibre of these two men to work with him on a regular basis.

In July 1870, Moody went to Indianapolis to participate in a YMCA convention. One of his duties was to speak at an early morning prayer meeting. Those gathered at that meeting were not encouraged to wipe the sleep from their eyes, for the singing was mournful and one brother prayed for what seemed an age.

During that prayer an immaculately dressed young man with mutton-chop whiskers entered, and took a seat near the door. The Rev Robert McMillen, a Presbyterian minister, recognised the newcomer and leaned over to him.

'The singing has been abominable. I wish you would start up something when that man stops, if he ever does,' he whispered.

Finally the prayer concluded and the young man immediately rose from his seat and began:

There is a fountain filled with blood,
Drawn from Immanuel's vein . . .

The assembly heard the stirring baritone voice and quickly joined in the hymn. D.L. Moody looked in the direction of the new song leader, and thanked God for the intervention.

After the meeting McMillen took the visitor to meet Moody, who was already approaching them. 'Mr Moody, I'd like you to meet Ira Sankey.'

D.L. shook Sankey's hand vigorously. 'Where are you from, Sankey?' he asked.

'Pennsylvania.'

'Are you married?' The questions came quickly.

'Yes.'

'Children?'

'Two.'

'What do you do for a living?'

Sankey began to wonder where the questions were leading. 'In Government service,' he replied.

'Well, you'll have to give that up.'

'Give it up? What for? Now it was Sankey's turn to do the asking.

'To come to Chicago to work with me.'

'But,' began the flummoxed singer, 'I can't leave my work just like that.'

'Sankey, I've been looking for the likes of you for eight years. I ain't gonna let you slip through my hands now,' persisted the evangelist. 'Join me in the vestry and we'll pray about it.'

The three men went to prayer. But Ira Sankey was adamant. He would not leave his job and join Moody. He confessed later that he only joined Moody for prayer out of politeness.

The next day Sankey received a card from Moody. It requested that the two meet on a specific street corner at six o'clock that evening. Sankey had only the barest idea of the purpose of the meeting, but just before six he turned up for the appointment with a few friends. D.L. was nowhere to be seen. But on the point of six he blustered onto the scene, acknowledged Sankey and his friends, and rushed into a store. A moment later he emerged carrying a packing case.

'Up you get, Sankey,' he commanded as he put the case down. 'Sing something.'

Sankey looked at the case and eyed the crowds streaming past on their way home from work. But with a smile he mounted the makeshift platform and launched forth into song. His companions joined in.

Astonished by this unexpected occurrence, the workers stopped their trek home, and a crowd quickly formed.

After concluding the hymn, Ira Sankey stepped down and D.L. climbed up on the box. It creaked under his weight.

'We are here today, men of Indianapolis, to tell you about the Lord Jesus,' he called out, and proceeded to preach the Gospel.

His new-found colleague recalled later, 'He preached that evening as I had never heard any man preach before.'

The crowd grew, and hemmed in the evangelist because of the lack of space. Recognising the limitations of their meeting place, Moody drew his sermon to a close, then announced, 'We are gonna hold another meetin' at the Academy of Music right away. Come with us.'

So saying, he dismounted from the case and, taking Sankey by the arm, began to march towards the hall. 'Sing again, Ira! Sing again!' Ira obliged with 'Shall we gather at the river?', and they and Sankey's friends led the way to their destination. The crowd after a moment's hesitation began to follow. The Gospel was presented again at the Academy of Music.

After the meeting they met with some associates to discuss a scheduled subject: 'How shall we reach the masses?' Moody and Sankey had already found one way.

Sankey returned home to New Castle with a troubled mind. The challenge to work in Chicago with Moody would not leave him. But the security of his present position seemed preferable to the risk of the one proposed. Over the succeeding weeks he discussed the matter with his wife, Fanny.

Early next year Moody suggested that Sankey join him for a week as a trial. So Ira Sankey journeyed to Chicago and worked alongside the vigorous Moody, and knew he was left with no choice. He resigned from his employment and joined the Illinois Street Church as a full-time worker.

Reflecting later on the six months between his first meeting with Moody and the subsequent one, Sankey said, 'I presume I prayed one way and he prayed another. However, it took him only six months to pray me out of business.'

Ira David Sankey was born in Edinburgh, Pennsylvania, on 28th August, 1840. Unlike his future companion, he was brought up in the home of a wealthy Methodist family. His father David was a member of the Pennsylvania Legislature. Like Moody's, his family was large. He had four brothers and four sisters.

Because he was a prominent member of the community the elder Sankey was frequently invited to attend services at churches of other denominations. Ira often accompanied him. This gave him a broader mind with regard to differences among Christians than was common at that time, and prepared him well for his future work.

An early major influence on his life was a Scottish farmer, whose holy life made a deep impact on the boy. The Scot used to take the young Sankey to Sunday School, as well as teach him.

From very early his musical talent was apparent. He loved singing, and any new tune he heard he could whistle or sing without a second hearing. He even began to compose tunes in his mid-teens.

A crusade was held at his church when he was fifteen, and he found himself under deep conviction of sin. In meeting after meeting he felt the convicting power of the Holy Spirit. Day after day a spiritual struggle ensued. At one meeting an elderly church member urged him to go forward with the inquirers. Sankey refused. The next night the drama was re-enacted with the same result. But the dear brother was persistent, and eventually Ira Sankey went forward. Yet it was not until a few days later that he experienced the release of sins forgiven and the joy of fellowship with Christ.

Shortly after his conversion his family moved to New Castle, where he became a member of the Jefferson Street Methodist Episcopal Church. He became the Superintendent of the Sunday School when he was twenty, and it was in this ministry that he began to 'sing the Gospel'. The Sunday School grew rapidly, and parents who brought their children along stayed to listen to the impressive baritone, rather than return home.

He also conducted a mid-week class for adults, a responsibility which caused him to search the Scriptures fervently, that he might be able to instruct them adequately. Some nights over sixty men and women attended the group to encourage, to share experiences, to pray and to study the Word.

He instructed his class to 'Tell us your condition in Bible language. The Scriptures abound with accounts of religious feeling. There is no state of grace which may not be described by a text.'

But his venture into such activities was interrupted when the Civil War began. Here again his life, at least initially, moved in a different direction from that of Moody. He enlisted in the northern army. But Ira Sankey was not a great success as a soldier. One night while on sentry duty he burst forth into song, his fine voice carrying far in the night air. He was totally oblivious of the fact that a Confederate sniper had him in his sights. But the southerner was so moved by the beautiful singing that he was unable to fire.

That God overruled in this situation is clear. Sankey's life was spared, not just for Sankey's sake but for the sake of those who were to come to the Lord through his ministry in later years, and for the glory of God.

His term of enlistment was for three months, and when that concluded he joined the Civil Service as a collector of internal revenue.

For the first half of 1871 the two evangelists teamed well, and their congregation continued to grow. Moody preached and Sankey sang, and all seemed well on the surface. But Moody was restless. He was involved in so many ministries that he seemed unsure which ones to favour. To most of his congregation nothing was amiss, but two women noticed his confusion and seeming dependence upon his own strength. They realised he needed to be filled with the Holy Spirit.

D.L. had the remarkable ability of being able to detect what was going on in all parts of an auditorium in which he was preaching. Little seemed to escape his attention. It is not surprising, therefore, that he observed 'Auntie' Sarah Cooke and Mrs Hawxhurst in the front pew praying while he was preaching one Sunday. At first he supposed they were praying for the unsaved, but something about their manner made him feel uneasy.

After the service he asked them what they were praying about.

'We were praying for you,' said the drably dressed 'Auntie'.

This was ridiculous, thought Moody. 'Why don't you pray for the people?' he asked grumpily.

'Because you need the power of the Spirit,' they answered in unison.

Moody was shocked. 'I need the power?' He looked about him at the large building and the hundreds of people wending their way home after listening to him.

'Yes, you need the power of God. You are too dependent upon yourself,' replied 'Auntie'.

Moody, feeling uncomfortable, drew the interview to a close and went home. During the next few weeks he thought little about the incident. But the two women met regularly in prayer with one issue in mind, that their beloved pastor should be filled with the power of God's Holy Spirit.

Gradually D.L. became concerned about the matter. 'Am I trusting in my own strength?' he asked himself. 'Certainly I often seem to lack power.'

Each time he met the two, they made it clear they were still praying for him. His spirit became troubled, and he asked if he might meet with them regularly for prayer. This they did, and Moody began to experience agony of soul as he poured out his heart to God asking to be 'baptised with fire' for his ministry.

On Sunday, 8th October, he preached in Farwell Hall, the

massive YMCA building named after his friend John. He preached on 'What shall I do with Jesus?' He concluded his message with the words: 'Now I want you to take the question with you and think it over, and next Sunday I want you to come back and tell me what you are going to do with him.'

As Moody finished and sat down, Sankey began to play on his little harmonium and launched into song.

> *Today the Saviour calls.*
> *Ye wanderers come;*
> *Oh, ye benighted souls,*
> *Why longer roam?*

He reached the third verse with a vague awareness of noise outside the building, but pressed on.

> *Today the Saviour calls.*
> *For refuge fly;*
> *The storm of justice falls,*
> *And death is nigh.*

The noise from the Chicago streets had risen in volume. The sound of fire engines rushing past, church bells ringing and the mad babble of shouting voices encroached upon Sankey's singing.

Sankey looked at Moody. D.L. rose from his seat and hastily pronounced the benediction. The congregation quickly dispersed. The two evangelists left through the back door, and saw the sky red with fire in the south-west. From across the river they heard the noise of madly galloping horses, people running and calling in panic, the sound of bells and the rush of wind. They parted company. Moody crossed the river to join his family. Sankey, his family safely in Pennsylvania, returned to the Hall. This was the first of several return visits that Ira Sankey made that evening to the Farwell Hall to salvage some personal belongings. When he left it for the final time, the building itself was well alight. He then retreated to the side of Lake Michigan where he endeavoured to comfort the refugees.

The firefighters were battling against impossible odds. The fire was too widespread and the winds too fierce for them to be able to contain it with their limited manpower and equipment. The fire spread rapidly and destructively.

D.L., meanwhile, made his way home. by the time he arrived it was obvious that much of the city would be destroyed. His fretting wife greeted him with relief. Her husband cried out, 'The city's doomed.' They entered the house, and peered out of the windows to try to determine if they were in any immediate danger.

The direction of the wind caused them to relax a little, but they realised that the Illinois Street church was in danger of being engulfed. Moody ventured out again, went to the church and began to retrieve items of value from the church office. By the time he returned to his family, Illinois Street church was a mass of flames.

In the part of town where the Moodys lived an air of relief pervaded the population as the conflagration appeared to be passing them by. Some went to bed. Others sat up to watch the once-in-a-lifetime spectacle.

In the early hours of the following morning the sound of urgent knocking could be heard. It was the police. The Moodys and their neighbours must be evacuated at once. Emma quickly dressed their two children, the younger Emma, who was nearly seven, and the two year old, Will. The children were driven to safety by a neighbour in a buggy, while the parents, pushing a pram containing a few belongings, escaped on foot. Their home was burned to the ground. Sankey, meanwhile, was in the safest place of all, in a boat on Lake Michigan. By the time it was under control, the fire had killed about 300 people, destroyed over 17,000 buildings and left over 90,000 homeless. He never again gave a congregation a week to think over their need of salvation.

Chapter 7

After the Chicago fire, Moody found himself in the forefront of relief work, as help slowly came in from surrounding areas. But a dispute arose over his methods of distributing supplies to the needy, so he decided to leave that aspect of the work to others. He then embarked on a whistle-stop tour of the major cities of America's east coast to raise funds to recommence his work.

But D.L.'s heart was no longer in fund raising. Instead he had a burning desire to know God more. The prayers of 'Auntie' Cooke and Mrs Hawxhurst were being answered. While in New York he paced the streets begging God to fill him with the Holy Spirit.

One day, no different from any other, he was walking along Fifth Avenue (or Broadway – he couldn't remember which), when he was overwhelmed by the presence of God. He rushed to the home of a friend nearby and informed him, 'I want to be alone. Let me have a room where I can lock myself in.' The astonished man obliged. Moody entered the room, locked the door and bathed in the glory of God.

The occurrence was so holy and precious to him that he very rarely spoke of it in later years. On one occasion when he did he said, 'It was almost too sacred an experience to name – Paul had an experience of which he never spoke for fourteen years – I can only say God revealed himself to me. I had such an experience of his love that I had to ask him to stay his hand.'

Moody continued his tour, preaching and asking for aid for the work in Chicago. His sermons had not changed, but his preaching had. Whereas before a handful were converted under his ministry, now hundreds were finding the Lord.

When he returned to Chicago, makeshift dwellings were scattered throughout what so short a time before had been a proud city. A temporary structure, the North Side Tabernacle, had been erected for worship near the site of the Illinois Street Church.

Services recommenced and thousands came. The Lord's Supper was held every Sunday at nine in the morning, preaching services at ten-thirty and seven-thirty, and Sunday School at three. God blessed abundantly. Over the next few months hundreds sought deliverance from sin.

But Moody was still restless. God was calling his Spirit-filled servant in a new direction. In the spring of 1872 he visited England again alone. Sankey was left in charge of the new church. While Moody was overseas his friend Sankey experienced a filling of the Spirit of God which made a radical change to his ministry. He became much more particular about the wording of the songs he sang, and many were brought to the Lord simply through his singing of the Word.

Moody's reasons for going to Britain were to rest and learn. 'I was determined not to get into work if I could help it,' he confided later. But resting was not Moody's strong point. He preached frequently and many noted that he was a man with a true gift from God.

While in Dublin he met an Englishman named Henry Varley. He enjoyed fellowship with Varley and his little band of Plymouth Brethren. One day, when the two men were out walking, Varley floored D.L. with a comment which continued to pound through Moody's mind weeks later. 'The world has yet to see what God will do through a man fully consecrated to him.'

'A man,' thought Moody, 'not an educated man or a great man, but a man, any man "fully consecrated to him." Oh, how I long to be that man. Make me that man, Lord,' he prayed.

On one Sunday he preached, morning and evening, in

a Congregational church in north London. The morning service was dead, and Moody wondered what he was doing there. It seemed almost a waste of time. But the evening service was totally different. The atmosphere was electric. The Spirit of God was at work. When he concluded his sermon he called out, 'I know that God is here and he has been working among us tonight. I ask that all those who want to become Christians to stand, so that we can counsel you and pray for you.'

Immediately people began to rise from all sections of the church. Within a matter of seconds dozens were standing. Still more rose to their feet, fifty, a hundred, more. D.L. was staggered. Perhaps they have misunderstood me, he thought. Surely not this many can be converted at once.

He decided to make his appeal clearer and more demanding. 'Now everyone who wants to become a Christian step into the inquiry room,' he said, indicating a hall next to the church. 'Just those who want to become Christians, no one else.'

Straight away people began to edge their way to the aisles. Quickly the aisles filled with crowds of people making their way to the rapidly filling room. Moody still couldn't believe it, nor could the pastor, Mr Lessey, and the leaders of the church. Such scenes were completely outside the experience of all of them.

After some time they managed to seat all the inquirers. But the evangelist was still cautious. 'I want everyone who wants to become a Christian to rise.' The noise was like thunder as the total assembly rose, pushing chairs and jostling for space.

Now what do we do? thought D.L. It will be impossible to counsel all these tonight. So he spoke to the pastor. It was decided that Moody would speak a few words of general counsel and pray for the inquirers, and invite them all back the following night.

The next day Moody had to return to Dublin. On Tuesday he received urgent word from Mr Lessey, advising that on Monday night there had been even more inquirers than on the Sunday. He went back to London without delay and preached on the next ten days at the same church. Four hundred people were added to that church as a result of that campaign.

Before embarking for America, D.L. was invited to return to England by a Methodist layman, Cuthbert Bainbridge. Bainbridge was a wealthy man, and he promised to support Moody if he came back to conduct evangelistic meetings.

When the evangelist arrived back in Chicago he received a further invitation from the Rev William Pennefather, an Anglican from north London.

Moody was in no doubt that he must return to England, and why not this time take Sankey with him. The preacher was convinced that it was a good idea. The singer was not.

Ira had been approached by Philip Phillips to join him in a series of singing engagements on the west coast. Phillips had made a very attractive offer to him, promising a handsome salary plus expenses. And now here was Moody urging a partnership in another land with no written financial guarantee. So he went to prayer.

For a while it seemed like no contest. To work with Phillips would be in God's service, so why not join him. But the doubts began to come. The Holy Spirit was at work. Sankey discussed the issue with a friend who advised, 'Don't go with Mr Phillips. Two workers in the same line, and especially two singers, are certain not to agree. Go with Moody, then you can do your work and he can do his.'

Finally he decided. 'D.L., I'll go with you to England.'

Chapter 8

Moody made it clear to his church in Chicago that it was his intention to leave them for a while to preach the Gospel in Britain. Not all were in sympathy with his intentions. John Farwell tried to persuade him to stay. 'Chicago needs you,' he said. Others felt that with Chicago still in the process of being rebuilt his timing for such a venture was completely wrong.

But Moody, though still concerned about Chicago, felt called to a wider mission field. He had received a further invitation from Britain, this time from George Bennett of the YMCA in York. He was left in no doubt as to his direction.

During the late winter and spring of 1873 he obtained a site for a new permanent building to replace the Illinois Street Church, and launched an appeal for funds to erect it. He and Sankey then began to prepare for their trip to Britain.

Of the three invitations received, D.L. had only seen fit to reply to one. He wrote to George Bennett advising him that he was thinking of making the trip and, if he did, would certainly spend time in York.

Shortly before they were due to leave Moody was accosted by 'Auntie' Cooke. It was clear she had doubts about his mission on the other side of the Atlantic. 'Are you going to preach to the miserable poor?' she snapped at him.

D.L. looked at her and thought for a moment. 'Yes,' he replied, 'and to the miserable rich too.'

'Auntie's' doubts were removed. Her beloved pastor was not sailing the seas for pleasure. D.L. Moody meant business.

On 7th June, 1873, Moody, his wife and children, and Ira and Fanny Sankey left New York on the *City of Paris* bound for Liverpool. The Sankeys, not expecting a lengthy stay, decided to leave their children with relatives.

On arrival in Britain they were dismayed to learn that both Bainbridge and Pennefather had died since inviting them to come. They went to George Bennett in York.

Bennett was pleased to see them, but embarrassed. He knew it would take some time for his American friends to be accepted by their English hearers. He regretted the total lack of preparation. But they made their plans quickly.

On Sunday morning, 22nd June, Moody and Sankey's British campaign started in a most modest way. Eight people met for prayer in a room at the YMCA. On to Salem Chapel they went. The church was full, but the mood was unsympathetic. Moody's American accent jarred on English ears.

But the lack of success did nothing to quench Moody's enthusiasm. He was now going full bore. Sankey and Bennett were less hearty as they walked in the direction of the Corn Exchange that afternoon.

On the way D.L. insisted that they stop at the YMCA to pick up some Bibles. He gave a pile to each of his friends and picked up another himself.

'What do you want all these for?' asked Bennett.

'You'll see. You'll see,' chuckled D.L., striding out in front, his two colleagues following on.

Though there had been little time for publicity, there were still hundreds of people present in the hall. As the three entered the building, Moody pulled some pieces of paper from his pocket and began to insert them in the Bibles. He then began to distribute the Bibles around the hall. As he gave each one he said to the recipient, 'When I call your number read this text out.' He indicated the numbers and references on the slips of paper.

When it was time for him to preach, he did so very informally, encouraging the sometimes reluctant members of the congregation to read the appropriate verses. The meeting was not a failure. Nor was it a roaring success.

Moody was feeling confident. His trust was in God. Some of his enthusiasm was beginning to rub off on his two friends. But they could think of no logical reason for confidence, just a growing inner conviction that something special would happen.

Meetings continued at various churches throughout the following week and into the next. All of them were marked by a little obvious response. Moody did not seem to be reaching his hearers, yet the novelty of Sankey accompanying his own singing on the harmonium had an increasing appeal to his listeners.

On Wednesday evening, 2nd July, Moody and Sankey found themselves in a large Wesleyan chapel. At first there was no reason to suppose that this meeting would be different from those that had preceded it.

When Moody preached he chose the subject of the blood of Christ. Starting in Exodus 12 and going through Scripture he traced the significance of blood in salvation.

'My friends, it was the blood that did it,' he began. 'God says, "When I see the blood I will pass over you. The blood shall be a token unto you." And I tell you, my friends, the greatest question that can be before you tonight is this: Have you got the token? Have you got the blood? Are you sheltered behind the precious blood of the Lamb? That is the question.'

He spoke slowly at first, but as he warmed to his task the words began to flow.

'People say: "If I were only as good as that minister, who has been preaching for fifty years, I should feel *so* safe." ' He emphasised the 'so'. ' "If I could give as much money to poor people as so-and-so gives, I should feel so safe for heaven." ' He repeated his emphasis. 'Let me say to you, my friends, if you are behind the blood of Jesus Christ, you are just as safe as any man or woman in the world. It is the blood.' His voice rose in volume.

'It ain't our good deeds. They don't save us from the curse of death. We must be sheltered behind the blood, and know that we are there, before we can be safe. Then the moment we are safe it will be time to talk about work.

'When you go to the railway station, and you buy a ticket, and get into a carriage; and the guard comes round and cries, "Tickets!" You pull out the ticket from your pocket and present it to him. The guard does not look to see if you are a white man or a black, learned or unlearned, great or small. He does not know who you are or what you are, but he looks for the token.

'Oh! my friends, God says, "If you have the token I will pass over you." Have you got the token? Young lady, have you got the token?' He stabbed a finger to the right of the church. 'Young man, have you got the token?' This time he pointed to the left.

Each one seemed to see those fingers pointing at him or her individually. Some fidgeted in embarrassment on the hard wooden pews. Moody was aware that his audience was beginning to respond. He continued to proclaim his subject. Old and New Testament Scriptures were quoted to hammer his points home. The congregation was absorbed in this message from the strange American preacher.

He began to draw his message to a close. 'My friends, what will you do with the precious blood tonight? Young lady, will you get up and leave this place, laughing and making light of the Son of God? Young man, will you turn with contempt from the Saviour and refuse a share in the great salvation he offers to you?' Again the fingers pointed. Consciences were being pricked. Sinners were coming under conviction.

'Some men seem to think it is noble to fight against such a Saviour; others have not the moral courage to lift up their voices for him. It is cowardice not to confess Christ after what he has done for us.

'Many years ago, when the Californian gold fever broke out, there was a great rush to the place. There was a young man who left a wife and little boy, and went to California. He told his wife that, as soon as he succeeded in business,

47

he would send for them. It was a long time before that letter came, and they received it with delight. They went to New York and took their passage in one of those beautiful Pacific steamers.

'They had not been out to sea long when, one beautiful day, when everything seemed calm and still, all at once there was a cry of "Fire! Fire!" The pumps were set to work, but the flames increased. There was a magazine of powder on board, and the captain knew the moment the fire touched it all would perish. The lifeboats were lowered, and the strongest of the passengers and crew sprang into them, leaving the rest to die. The last lifeboat was being lowered, and the mother begged the crew to take her and the boy. They refused. She pleaded with them. At last they promised to take one of them.

'What do you think she did?' Moody paused to let the question sink in. 'Did the mother leap into the boat and leave the boy to perish? No true mother would do that. This mother seized her darling boy; she pressed him to her heart and handed him over the side. As she dropped him into the boat she said, "My son, if you live to see your father, tell him that I died in your place." The boat pushed off, and in a little while the steamer was blown up. The mother perished.' His voice seemed to choke as his illustration reached its climax. Tears were in his eyes.

'Young men, what would you say of that son, who is now grown up, if he should speak disrespectfully of such a mother as that? You would say he weren't fit to live.

'Ah, Christ has done more than that for you.' He pointed again. 'He left a life of glory to endure a life of shame; while we were without strength, he died for us. He did not die for his friends alone; he died also for his enemies. I want you all to come to him tonight. Won't you believe in him and be saved?'

The congregation was silent except for the sound of a few sniffing into handkerchiefs.

'Now I want all who want to have their lives changed by the power of God through faith in Jesus Christ as a personal Saviour to stand.'

Immediately several rose, then more.

'Would all those,' he emphasised the all, 'who want to become Christians rise?'

More stood up. Some were openly crying.

'My friend Ira Sankey is now going to sing a hymn. While he is singing, there is still time for you to stand. When he has finished we will go into the inquiry room,' he indicated an adjoining hall, 'where you will be counselled.'

The sound of the harmonium was heard and Sankey began to sing in gentle tones:

Just as I am – without one plea
But that Thy blood was shed for me,
And that Thou bidd'st me to come to Thee,
O Lamb of God, I come.

More of the congregation did 'come' as they rose to their feet.

Sankey concluded his singing and the inquirers were ushered into the room for counselling.

One of the church's leaders was so overcome at the sight of the largest harvest that church had seen in living memory, that he broke down in tears of joy.

Chapter 9

On their first Monday in York, George Bennett had introduced the two visitors to a serious-looking young man. 'Mr Meyer, may I introduce the two American gentlemen I told you about, Mr D.L. Moody and Mr Ira Sankey. Gentlemen, this is Frederick Meyer.'

F.B. Meyer shook hands with the two newcomers. He was formally polite, but showed no enthusiasm. Moody was his usual irrepressible self, greeting Meyer warmly. Sankey was a little hesitant.

'Mr Meyer is the minister at the Baptist church where you will be preaching on Sunday,' advised Bennett.

'We will be glad to visit your church, Mr Meyer,' enthused D.L.

The Baptist pastor was nonplussed. He had only agreed to allow the two Americans to take part in the services in his church as a favour to George Bennett. He was too polite to tell his visitors that he would not be 'glad' to have them in his church, but too honest to give a false impression. 'Till next Sunday then, gentlemen,' he said and walked off.

During the week he expressed to Bennett that he failed to see what these two men could do that he couldn't. The YMCA man was disappointed in his friend's attitude, but he did not try to change it.

Sunday came and the two evangelists led the services. Meyer was at first unimpressed. But what did finally leave its mark on him was the effect Moody and Sankey had on some of his congregation. The Englishman noted that some had been significantly influenced by the visitors, particularly one Sunday School teacher. This young woman led her entire class to Christ that Sunday afternoon.

He was now sufficiently open-minded to invite Moody and Sankey back when their commitments at the Wesleyan chapel had concluded. For two weeks, night after night at the new Baptist church 'Moody preached the Gospel and Sankey sang the Gospel' to ever enlarging congregations. When no empty pews remained, people sat on the stairs and in the vestibule area, so keen was their desire to hear the Word.

F.B. Meyer's attitude changed dramatically. Years later he was to remember: 'For me it was the birth-time of new conceptions of ministry, new methods of work, new inspirations and hopes. I learned the psychology of the soul. I learned how to point men to God.'

On 19th July, the two evangelists and their families moved north to the shipbuilding town, Sunderland. Their five weeks there began discouragingly, though attendance at the meetings increased towards the end. But the ministers of most churches were suspicious of their methods, which limited their opportunities. Moody said, 'We never can go on in this way. It is easier fighting the devil than the ministers.' Eventually, they decided to call it a day and went on to Newcastle-upon-Tyne.

After overcoming the initial suspicions of the Christians of Newcastle, their work was greatly blessed by God. Ministers from a variety of denominations invited them to their churches, and, for the first time, the Church of England showed support. Moody and Sankey laboured for more than ten weeks in that coal-mining town with results that radiated far beyond the boundaries of the city.

While in Newcastle, Moody and Sankey received an invitation to conduct meetings in Scotland. Two Scots, the Rev John Kelman and the Rev James Hood-Wilson, issued the invitation, and at the end of November the evangelists arrived in Edinburgh.

A hot welcome in Scotland was more likely than a warm one. For in no other part of the British Isles was there likely to be more opposition to their methods. The land of the 'bonnie heather' boasted many fine, doctrinally sound preachers, and an unordained 'amateur' such as D.L. Moody would inevitably be viewed with suspicion. Traditionally in Scottish churches singing in the services was unaccompanied. Organs were regarded as an abomination. Solos were outlawed, and psalms were sung, not hymns. Moody was less confident than usual and Sankey was distinctly nervous.

But there were those in Scotland who, like Kelman and Wilson, recognised that much of Scottish Christianity had become coldly formal. The churches of Scotland needed a breath of fresh air, or, more accurately, the divine wind of the Holy Spirit.

Upon arrival the Moodys went to stay with Professor William Blaikie. Ira and Fanny Sankey were hosted by the hymn-writer, Horatius Bonar. It was a stormy night, and D.L. became sick with tonsillitis.

Sunday came and D.L. could scarcely speak. Preaching was out of the question. For several weeks in advance prayer meetings had been held to prepare for the coming campaign. Publicity had been widespread, with news coming across the border of mighty happenings in Newcastle. Many people were looking forward to hearing Moody and Sankey for themselves. But for the first meeting in the Music Hall it was to be Sankey without Moody.

Ira Sankey had spent long enough in the public service to know the value of diplomacy. He commenced the service with a metric psalm, the Old Hundredth:

> All people that on earth do dwell,
> Sing to the Lord with cheerful voice . . .

The congregation sang the familiar strains well. Even Sankey's severest critic would not frown on that opening. He then felt enough freedom to follow it with 'Jesus of Nazareth passeth by'. The Rev J.H. Wilson preached in Moody's absence.

The next night D.L. was sufficiently recovered to preach at Wilson's Barclay Free Church, but Sankey did not participate. His harmonium was out of action, being damaged when falling from a cab transporting it to the church. He refused to sing without it.

It was not until the third night that the two evangelists worked in tandem in Scotland. There were those who still frowned on the 'kist fu' o' whistles', as they had nicknamed Sankey's little portable organ. But the crowd packing Barclay Free Church was so large that many had to stand. Night after night the crowds kept coming.

Invitations came from other Edinburgh churches. Moody preached, Sankey sang and souls were saved wherever they went. The news of their campaign began to spread throughout Scotland, and invitations began to come from further afield. In the New Year they went from Edinburgh to Dundee and then to Glasgow.

The Glasgow campaign commenced on 8th February, 1874. Services were held in various churches, in the City Hall, and eventually in the giant Kibble Palace, situated in the Botanic Gardens. Wherever they went the auditoriums were packed, the inquiry rooms busy.

When all was going so well, Satan attacked. A letter arrived from a lawyer in America accusing Moody of impropriety in business. D.L. was distraught. This could wreck everything, he thought. He quickly penned a letter to John Farwell seeking help to clear his name. John Kelman, one of Moody's original supporters in Scotland, also wrote to Farwell requesting confirmation or denial of the lawyer's letter.

The reply was a long time coming but the crusade continued unabated. Though the letter had been circulated widely, few seemed to believe it. Most were so impressed by the preacher's transparent honesty, that they were sure its contents were false. Eventually a letter arrived from Chicago, signed by over thirty of that city's clergy, clearing Moody's name.

'We the undersigned, Pastors of the City of Chicago,' read the letter, 'learning that the Christian character of D.L. Moody has been attacked, hereby certify that his labours in the YMCA, and as an evangelist in this city have been Evangelical and Christian in the highest sense of those terms.

We do not hesitate to commend him as an earnest Christian worker, worthy of the confidence of our Scotch and English brethren.'

On 20th May, the two evangelists were on a train returning to Edinburgh to conduct a few more meetings there. Moody was reading a batch of letters just received from America; Sankey was engrossed in a Christian magazine. As the singer turned the pages he saw a heading, 'The Lost Sheep'. Beneath it was a poem. He read it and was deeply moved. When he had recovered sufficiently he said to his companion, 'There's a poem here, D.L., which would make a fine hymn, if it had a tune.'

'Read it then, Sankey. Read it,' D.L. urged without looking up from the letter he was reading.

Sankey complied with the request. He scarcely looked up as he read the verses. When he had finished he looked at Moody. 'Well, what do you think?'

No answer came. Moody's thoughts were back in Chicago. He hadn't heard a word. Sankey was not impressed – If he wanted me to read it, he could at least have had the decency to listen, he thought, but said nothing. He tore the poem from the magazine and put it in his coat pocket.

The next day they participated in a meeting in the multi-towered Free Church Assembly Hall. Moody chaired the meeting, but did not preach. That was left to a few of the ministers gathered for the occasion. They had all concentrated on the theme 'The Good Shepherd'. When the final speaker, Horatius Bonar, had concluded, Moody turned to his colleague seated at the organ.

'Have you got a suitable solo, to end with, Ira?' he asked.

The singer-evangelist was floored. What could he sing? The Twenty-Third Psalm? No, that had already been sung at that meeting. If only there was a tune to the poem 'The Lost Sheep', that would be most suitable. But there wasn't, though during the previous twenty-four hours an appropriate melody had begun to form in his mind.

He fumbled in his pocket and pulled out the scrap of paper.

He placed it on the organ, and nervously began to fiddle with his moustache. 'Can I do it or not?' he asked himself. He quickly offered a silent prayer to God, and launched forth in song.

> *There were ninety and nine that safely lay*
> *In the shelter of the fold,*
> *But one was out on the hills away,*
> *Far off from the gates of gold –*
> *Away on the mountains wild and bare,*
> *Away from the tender Shepherd's care,*
> *Away from the tender Shepherd's care.*

Not a sound could be heard but Sankey's voice and the 'kist fu' o' whistles'. Moody could feel a lump in his throat, and a tear began to run down his cheek.

Sankey continued, his rich baritone reaching every corner of the hall.

> *'Lord, Thou hast here Thy ninety and nine;*
> *Are they not enough for Thee?'*
> *But the Shepherd made answer: 'This is Mine*
> *Has wandered away from Me;*
> *And although the road be rough and steep,*
> *I go to the desert to find my sheep,*
> *I go to the desert to find my sheep'.*

The singer continued with the remaining verses, and, in the rare moments he dared look up from the keyboard, he could see many in the congregation dabbing their eyes with handkerchiefs.

When he had concluded, Moody walked to him and peered through tear-filled eyes at the slip of paper on the harmonium.

'Where did you find that hymn, Ira?' he asked. 'It was beautiful.'

'That was the poem I read to you on the train, but you didn't listen then,' replied his friend pointedly.

Moody smiled and patted the singer on the shoulder.

The poem of the recently deceased Elizabeth Clephane

had not only found a tune, but had struck a chord which was to echo throughout Victorian Britain.

A further problem which arose during their work in Britain concerned the different traditions of hymnology followed by the Americans and the British. It was fine for Sankey to sing songs previously unknown to British ears, but if he wanted the congregation to join in they had to painstakingly be taught the words and music. For the most part the hymnbooks used in British churches did not contain the words and music used by the American singer.

Sankey had these songs in a musical scrapbook which he used at the meetings. He was frequently asked to loan the book, but was reluctant to do so in case it was lost or not returned in time for a meeting.

It became clear that they needed their own hymnbook for use in their work. While in the north of England, Sankey met an English publisher named R.C. Morgan, who said he would be happy to publish a songbook for him. So Sankey cut out twenty-three songs from his scrapbook and wrote on them: 'Sacred Songs and Solos sung by Ira D. Sankey at the meetings of Mr Moody of Chicago.'

Within two weeks 500 copies of the little hymnal complete with music arrived safely in Sankey's hands. Priced at sixpence each they sold out on the first day, and had to be hurriedly reprinted in a much larger quantity. Later a words-only edition arrived. These were sold for a penny each.

Accusations that Moody and Sankey were 'in it for the money' were increasingly common, and their opponents saw in the hymnbook some apparent justification for that belief. Unwilling to be seen as making money out of the Gospel, they decided to channel the royalties into the rebuilding of the Chicago Avenue Church.

Sacred Songs and Solos went on to become a hymbook with 1,200 songs, including many traditional hymns, but majoring in songs with a peculiarly Victorian ethos. It became known to several generations of Evangelicals simply as 'Sankey's'.

Chapter 10

At the end of May they began a tour of northern Scotland, holding campaigns in Perth, Dundee, Aberdeen, Inverness and other smaller towns. For a brief while in August, Sankey journeyed south to be reunited with his wife, who had just had a baby, and his other children, recently arrived from America. Moody soldiered on alone.

In September the evangelists crossed the Irish Sea and began holding services in Belfast. So great was the impact that after one open-air meeting counsellors laboured from two p.m. till ten that evening dealing with those troubled about their spiritual condition. At another service 200 men were converted.

But if such scenes in the largely Protestant north could be understood, the successes which followed in the Catholic south came as a surprise to all.

In Dublin the meetings were held in the Exhibition Palace, where thousands of Protestants, Catholics and those of no faith attended.

The Catholic Prelate, Cardinal Cullen, was so concerned at the number of his flock going to the crusades that he issued an interdict forbidding their attendance. It had little effect.

At the end of 1874 the evangelists returned to England, and proclaimed the Gospel through the winter months in Manchester, Sheffield, Birmingham and Liverpool.

But the main challenge lay ahead – London. London was not just the capital of Britain, it was the world's major city. A vast metropolis of over five million people, including the very rich and the desperately poor. Moody was going to be true to his promise to 'Auntie' Cooke: he intended to reach both rich and poor for the Lord Jesus Christ.

The Gospel had been preached with great success in towns big and small throughout the British Isles. Wherever they went Moody and Sankey had become household names. But would they have such an impact in London?

Spurgeon was still proclaiming the Gospel to thousands every Sunday. William Booth was ten years into his work among the poverty-stricken East Enders. London did not lack for preachers, yet sin abounded. The Christianity of many was only skin deep, a mere Sunday religion. The need was there, and so was the call.

A committee had been formed in the capital, under the leadership of three laymen – Thomas Stone, Robert Paton and James Mathieson. It was decided to divide London into four sections and hold a series of meetings in each. On 9th March the first London meeting was held in the northern quarter. The venue was the enormous Agricultural Hall in Islington, normally the scene of horse and cattle shows. For the first few days an estimated 18,000 crammed into the hall. But because of the size of the buildings many were unable to hear, so the organisers partitioned off sections of the auditorium and reduced the seating capacity to 14,000.

One night the hall was filling rapidly and Moody was directing the seating arrangements, as was his habit. He stood on the platform especially erected to accommodate Moody, Sankey and various clergymen and dignitaries. As he was watching the crowd he noticed two elderly ladies trying to find vacant seats in the front. Just at that point, the crusade organiser, the Rev H.C. Billing, came up to D.L. accompanied by a well-dressed man.

'Oh, Mr Moody, may I introduce the Earl of Shaftesbury,' said Billing. 'Lord Shaftesbury, this is Dwight Moody.'

Moody looked at Billing, and then at the elderly philanthropist. 'Glad to meet you, Lord Shaftesbury,' he said, sticking out his giant fist and crushing the visitor's delicate hand. 'Can you see those two old ladies down there?' He pointed them out to the distinguished visitor.

Shaftesbury nodded.

'Well, we have more chairs than we need on the platform. Would you please take two down to them?'

Shaftesbury smiled and took the chairs. Billing blushed. D.L. kept on organising.

Sankey took his place at the organ, situated right next to the pulpit on the platform. The service began. Moody announced the first hymn and the hall erupted into song. Each member of the vast congregation held a copy of the little song book that the singer had compiled for the campaigns. Above their heads flickered hundreds of gas lights.

When the singing concluded, Moody led briefly in prayer, his voice carrying to the four corners of the enormous hall. He finished and directed his attention to the crowd massed before him. 'I know that many in this building tonight are Christians,' he said, 'and I have a brief word for you. Many Christians are noted for their lack of activity in the service of their Master. They are always waiting for something to happen before they do a job for God. Let me tell you this, my English brothers and sisters, don't wait for something to turn up. Go and turn something up.' Then, leaning towards his colleague seated beside him, he said, 'It's your turn now, Ira.'

Sankey fiddled with his moustache and then addressed the congregation. 'Towards the end of the "War between the States" so recently concluded, a war in which so many fine young men died, the brave northern troops were under siege at Allatoona in Georgia. They were heavily outnumbered and things looked black. But their spirits were cheered by a message from General Sherman: "Hold the fort; I am coming." Heroically they did hold on, and the day was saved. A friend of mine, Philip Bliss, wrote a hymn based on that incident. I will sing it to you.'

His fingers touched the keys of the organ and he launched into song.

Ho my comrades! see the signal
Waving in the sky!
Reinforcements now appearing,
Victory is nigh!

'Hold the fort, for I am coming?'
Jesus signals still;
Wave the answer back to heaven,
'By thy grace we will!'

Sankey continued through the song and encouraged the congregation to join in the chorus.

When it was time for D.L. to preach, the people were in full sympathy with the two American evangelists. Moody stood on the platform, Bible in hand, and addressed the throng.

'I am going to take for my text this evening, "a man"; the last one whom Jesus saved before he went back to heaven. And the fact that he saved such a man at all, ought to give every one of us a great deal of hope and comfort. This man was a thief, a highwayman, a murderer, perhaps, yet Christ takes him with him when he ascends to glory. If our Lord is not ashamed of such a man, surely no class of sinners need to feel that they are left out.' Moody knew well that before him sat sinners of every imaginable type.

He continued on his verbal journey, telling the story of Jesus on the cross and the two thieves crucified beside him. He then began to apply it. 'Here is one of the great difficulties with a great many people. They don't like to own that they are sinners. They excuse themselves in every way. They cover up the fact which this penitent thief confesses openly.'

Moody continued preaching, his voice the only one heard in that vast congregation. Every eye was on him. Every mind attentive to his words. He drew his address to a conclusion with an illustration: 'A little while ago, in one of the mining districts of England, a young man attended one of our meetings, and refused to go from the place till he had found peace in the Saviour. The next day he returned to the pit, and the coal fell upon him. When they took him out, broken and mangled, he had only two or three minutes of life left in him. As his friends gathered around, they saw his lips moving. Bending down, they heard him say, "It was a good thing I settled it last night."

'Settle it tonight, my friends, once for all,' challenged Moody. 'Begin now to confess your sins, and to pray the Lord to remember you when he cometh into his kingdom.'

The silence which followed was interrupted only by sobs from different parts of the auditorium. Then Sankey played the little organ and began to sing: 'There were ninety and nine that safely lay . . .'

Inquirers were numerous after the service and they were counselled in the gallery of the Agricultural Hall and in the nearby St Mary's Hall.

The crusade continued in the north London centre for five weeks, and when Moody and Sankey departed to conduct similar services in the eastern quarter of the city, other ministers continued the work in the northern part.

In the East End, the 10,000-seat Bow Road Hall had been erected especially for them. It proved to be too small, and a tent had to be set up beside it for 'overflow meetings'. The work proceeded as successfully here in the poorest part of London as it had in the more comfortably off north.

Chapter 11

From the 'miserable poor' Moody and Sankey went to the 'miserable rich', and commenced a series of meetings in the Royal Opera House, Haymarket. For much of the duration of the campaign in the East End, the two evangelists combined the two, holding a service nightly at seven-thirty at Bow Road, and then rushing westward to the Royal Opera House to hold another at nine o'clock.

The surroundings were vastly different. The splendour of the Opera House contrasted dramatically with the spartan fittings in the drab Bow Road Hall. The wealth and finery of the clientele in the west were so different from the poverty and rags of the East Enders. Moody felt comfortable preaching to both. He knew that all, rich or poor, had souls to save. Sankey, initially a little overawed by the Opera House, came to revel in it.

At first many of the rich attended the meetings as a form of entertainment. But the Holy Spirit overcame cynicism, and many who came to scoff stayed to repent. D.L.'s rough-and-ready speech amused his hearers; his passionate sincerity moved them to tears.

Each night the galleries and boxes were filled, apart from a few privately rented boxes, which were closed for the duration by lessees who disapproved of the non-theatrical activities. The audiences included many of the nobility, including members of the Royal Family. Sankey was impressed, but it all came the same to D.L.

During the campaign in the West End the first link was forged in a chain of events which was to have world-wide influence.

Edward Studd was a wealthy man. He owned a

magnificent mansion in Wiltshire and several racehorses. He was a heavy gambler. Late in May that year he played host in his London home to an old acquaintance named Vincent. Unknown to Studd his companion had become a Christian at a Moody and Sankey rally in Dublin a few months before. Studd promised that after dinner Vincent could decide their place of entertainment, to while away the evening hours.

After the meal Studd said, 'Well, my friend, what is it to be? The theatre, a concert maybe, or a game of cards? You do play, don't you?'

Vincent looked at him and smiled slightly. 'Why not the Royal Opera House?' he ventured.

'The Opera! What a splendid . . .' Studd's voice trailed off, but picked up again. 'But that's where those American fellows are. What are their names? Moody and Sankey,' he said, answering his own question. 'That would be like going to church, my dear Vincent. Church is for Sundays, not weekdays.'

'But Studd, you said the choice of entertainment was mine, and Moody and Sankey it is.'

The racing man was trapped. A gentleman couldn't go back on his word, so off they went to the Haymarket. By the time they had made their way through the dense traffic no empty seats remained in the hall. Studd was delighted, but Vincent was determined. Realising that his companion was unlikely to attend an evangelical gathering if he missed this one, he wrote a note to a friend on the committee and gave it to a steward.

They waited outside for a few minutes. Studd showed his irritation. Then Vincent's friend emerged from the hall, and, following introductions, invited them in. Studd's delight turned to gloom, but he had no choice but to co-operate.

His negative attitude gradually changed as D.L. preached. He felt that the evangelist's message was aimed directly at him. He went home in a disturbed state of mind. The next night he returned to the Opera House alone, and again, night after night. He couldn't stay away. Moody and Sankey did their work, and the Holy Spirit did the work which only he can do. Edward Studd became a Christian.

The next link in the chain began to be forged without Studd's knowledge. Eton College, the most famous of all English public schools, was where many English Prime Ministers, other politicians and senior civil servants had been educated. During the west London meetings one of the boys from Eton had been converted. Strongly desiring to share his blessings with his schoolmates, he invited the two Americans to conduct a service at the college. They consented. Among the scholars at Eton were three of Studd's sons, Kynaston, George and Charlie.

The plan was to erect a tent on land near the college, and hold a service especially for the Eton boys on Tuesday, 22nd June. The plan was simple enough. But Eton was high Church of England, and, to some, the idea of having unordained nonconformists preaching to the pick of the country's young men was outrageous.

The headmaster had given permission for the boys to attend, but refused to have the service linked in any way with the school. But it was obviously impossible to sever all connection. One parent, a Member of Parliament named Knatchbull-Hugessen, found out about it and launched a protest. His letters to *The Times* and *The Morning Post* caused an uproar. The headmaster was inundated with letters of objection from the parents of boys at the school and Old Etonians. The matter was discussed in the House of Lords with so much emotion and indignation that it seemed the future of the Empire was at stake.

The next step was for the Mayor of Windsor, an adjoining town, to offer the Windsor Town Hall for the service. But he withdrew his offer when he heard a rumour that some of the Eton boys had bought hundreds of eggs, the purpose of which one could well guess.

Finally, the service was held on private property in the open air. Nearly 200 of the boys attended; a handful of masters and several hundred parents and local residents joined them. In the congregation were Edward Studd and his sons. Moody's text, rather ironically, was 'Behold, I bring you glad tidings of great joy which shall be to all people.'

The three Studd boys had been astonished by the change they had seen in their father. From being a very worldly man, he had become a spiritual one, with a keen desire to see souls saved. Though they had co-operated with their father and gone with him to hear Moody and Sankey, the service made no lasting impression on them. But Edward Studd was a determined man. Young Christian though he was, he knew the importance of prayer, and he began to pray fervently for the salvation of his sons. Sometime later, unknown to each other, the three became Christians on the same day.

Early in the summer Moody and Sankey began their final series of meetings in London. Another temporary building had been constructed in south London and named the Camberwell Hall. Smaller than its counterpart in the East End, it still held a crowd of about 8,000. In the cool drizzly weather that masqueraded as a summer that year, the south Londoners journeyed to the hall in their thousands nightly. Overflow meetings in nearby churches accommodated those unable to find a spot in the packed hall.

They concluded their London campaigns at the Camberwell Hall on 13th July. Then, after a brief holiday, they left England on 4th August to return to their homeland.

The work which had begun so modestly in York in the middle of 1873 concluded in triumph in London two years later.

Chapter 12

The Moody and Sankey families arrived back in America on 14th August. Their reception in New York was noticeably different from that which greeted their arrival in England two years before. The press was out in strength, and so were the clergy of a variety of denominations. Their activities in Britain had been followed with growing interest on the other side of the Atlantic. The news of the way God had used them had spread throughout the USA. Invitations to conduct meetings in major American cities awaited them.

Their initial move was to retreat to D.L.'s old home in Northfield. His mother, now in her seventy-first year, greeted them warmly. Though she still disagreed with much of her son's doctrine, she was very proud of his achievements. Two of his brothers, Edwin and the twin Samuel, still lived at home.

D.L. received an invitation from the local Unitarian minister, Jabez Sunderland, to preach in his church on a convenient Sunday. But Moody refused. 'Unitarians insult Christ,' he stated, 'and he who insults Christ insults me.' He accepted, instead, an invitation to preach in the Trinitarian Church.

Betsey Moody, though proud of her son, had not yet heard him preach. She refused all invitations to attend the Trinitarian Church. Each time she replied, 'I'll remain a Unitarian 'til the day I die.' Then one Sunday quite out of the blue she joined the others in the family buggy, and went to hear her son.

That morning he preached on Psalm 51, David's psalm of penitence. At the conclusion of the message, Moody asked those wishing to trust in Christ as Saviour to stand. Among those who rose from the pews was the white-haired figure of his mother. The son was so overcome with emotion that he was unable to say a closing prayer, and gave that task to another minister.

A few days later, Dwight's youngest brother, Samuel became a Christian.

But it was impossible to keep the energetic Moody confined in Northfield, even though he had a new-found love for the town. God was calling him to a wider ministry. On 24th October he and Sankey began a series of meetings in New York.

Preparation for the services had been going on for some weeks, and the skating rink in Brooklyn had been hired for them. As had been found in England, the building, though it held 6,000 people, was not large enough. On some nights more were left outside than gained admittance. For some meetings Christians were persuaded to stay away so that opportunity could be given for more of the unconverted to attend.

After a month in New York they went to Philadelphia. Providentially one of Moody's old supporters, John Wanamaker, had just purchased the enormous Pennsylvania Railroad Depot for a business venture. He was delighted to let Moody and Sankey make good use of it during the closing weeks of that year and the first two in 1876. On the first night, in spite of rain and a major road being closed because of a fire, 10,000 attended. Night after night the hall was crowded. At the final meeting 13,000 packed the auditorium. Many more had to be turned away.

After a short break in Florida, Moody teamed up again with Sankey in New York. This time their preaching place was again the Gilmore Concert Garden. This venue had had a varied career, firstly as a railway station, then home of P.T. Barnum's circus when it was known as the Hippodrome, and it was later to be redeveloped as Madison Square Garden.

As with the crusades in Britain, preparations had been going on for months before the actual commencement on 7th February. A team of 500 ushers had been organised, a choir of over 600 assembled, and prayer meetings had been frequent.

About 7,000 attended the first meeting, and Moody, entering between the choir and the dignitaries on the massive platform, raised his hand for silence. 'Let us open the meeting in silent prayer,' he called out. The congregation bowed their heads and followed the evangelist's instructions, with a silence that could almost be felt. He then announced a hymn, at which point Sankey seated himself at the organ, began playing and led the vast crowd in an enthusiastic hymn. Thus began one of the most important religious campaigns in American history.

The eyes of most of the nation were upon New York, the country's largest city. People from all Christian persuasions and those without Christian convictions watched with interest as night after night, day after day, thousands made their way to the 'Hippodrome'. On some days as many as four meetings were held, and for ten weeks Moody preached and Sankey sang at women's meetings and meetings exclusively for men, as well as gatherings for all.

Thousands had their lives changed in a conversion to Christ, or a rekindling of faith in him. One church received nearly 140 new members that year, mainly converts made through the crusade. But the influence went wider as numerous Christians throughout America learned what God could do, not just through Moody and Sankey, but through anyone dedicated to Christ and suitably gifted by his Spirit. Even the *New York Times* recognised at the conclusion of the campaign that the morals of the city had been noticeably uplifted. J. Wilbur Chapman said, 'In moving New York God moved the country, and the voice of the evangelists was heard throughout the land.'

After New York, Moody went on a whistle-stop tour of the Mid-West, accompanied by the evangelist Major

Whittle, who previously had been conducting Moody and Sankey style meetings with Philip Bliss. The two men conducted numerous meetings in towns as far apart as Augusta, Nashville, St Louis, Kansas and Des Moines.

While this tour was going on preparations were in hand for another major campaign, this time in Chicago. Going through his mind were our Lord's words, 'A prophet is not without honour, save in his own country.' How would he be received after his seeming desertion of Chicago after the fire? He had also had to bear the worry of his son Willie's sickness. During the New York winter Willie had been taken seriously ill, and Emma took him south to the milder climate of Augusta.

But Moody need not have worried. Willie recovered, and the people of Chicago were enthusiastic about the return of 'their' travelling evangelist. The work in Chicago began on 1st October with meetings at the Tabernacle and the new Farwell Hall. He and Sankey were as well received there as they had been in most of Britain and their other ports of call in the USA.

If ever a man's name failed to describe his character, it was Moody's. A less moody man would have been hard to find, yet amidst all the success Moody found himself unusually joyless. On 6th October he dined with Whittle and confided that he sensed God was about to test him. The nature of the affliction he knew not, but that one was around the corner he felt sure.

The next day he was meeting with some Christian friends, when Whittle entered. 'There's some mail here for you, D.L., and a telegram,' he said. He took it to where Moody was seated and handed the envelopes to him. Moody looked at them and opened the telegram. As he read it he cried out as if in agony, stood suddenly, spilling the letters on the floor, and blurted out, 'Sam's dead!' He fell back into his chair, and wept uncontrollably. Sam, his favourite brother, had gone to be with his Lord, but D.L. felt the loss badly.

As he recovered from the initial shock of the news, he turned to Whittle and through trembling lips muttered,

'You'll have to take over here, Major. I'm going to Northfield.'

Whittle felt the desire to protest, but as he looked at Moody's tear-stained face he realised he couldn't. 'Yes, my friend, you go. We will do our best to carry on here until you return.'

So Moody hurried to Northfield, and Whittle and Sankey continued the crusade in his absence in Chicago.

After a week he returned, and continued the work right through into the New Year.

Before the end of the year, however, a further piece of sad news reached his ears. On 29th December the Pacific Express travelling through Ohio in a fierce storm plunged into a precipice when a bridge collapsed. On board was Philip Bliss. He had managed to climb out of the burning wreck, but went back to rescue his wife. Neither survived.

Chapter 13

On his tour through the Mid-West with Whittle, Moody gradually came to realise that he must have a settled base for his activities. The question was, where? Chicago and Northfield seemed the most likely candidates, but he found it unusually difficult to decide which. His week spent in Northfield for Sam's funeral settled the issue. His birthplace it was to be.

A few months before Sam's death, D.L. had spent a little time in Northfield. One day as the brothers were riding in a buggy, they turned a corner and came across a small house. The owner was sitting in the doorway. Moody reined in the horse and stopped near the man. They climbed down from the buggy and D.L. whispered to his brother, 'That isn't Horace Sikes, is it?'

'Yes, D.L.,' his brother confirmed, 'he suffers from paralysis now, and he and his family have a pretty tough time of it.'

Inside the house Sikes's two teenage daughters were making straw hats, the family's main source of income. Moody was all concern and questions. 'Do the girls go to school?' was one. The reply was in the negative, though Sikes, an ex-school-teacher, himself taught them as best he could within the limits of his own fitness and his daughters's lack of spare time.

After saying farewell to the family the two brothers returned home, with Sam holding the reins, at a much slower pace.

Sam had talked of a dream he had had for some time of a good quality girls' High School in Northfield, for girls whose families could not afford to educate them.

When Sam died, D.L. decided that the dream would become a reality.

After the Chicago crusade the evangelist held another in Boston. There Moody met Henry Durant, a retired lawyer who had opened a school for girls based on Christian principles. The following year a friend of Durant, H.N.F. Marshall, went to Northfield to help D.L. commence the project. Marshall purchased a sixteen-acre block of land near the Moody home, and later an adjoining block was added. The Northfield Seminary for Girls was finally opened in November 1879. Within a year 100 girls were being educated there.

So successful was the girls' school, that Moody decided to erect a similar institution for boys. Mt Hermon School for Boys opened in June 1881. Moody was determined that the children of Northfield and surrounding districts would have a better education than he.

During the period in which the schools were planned and built, Moody spent less time in public ministry, and more in study. He felt keenly his lack of education, and he spent much time studying the Bible. Moody was content for a while to be out of the public eye. Sankey, however, was keen to get back into action.

In the autumn Sankey called on his friend. After the usual pleasantries, Sankey came quickly to the point. 'D.L., I think it's time we went back to England. We have had any number of invitations, and I don't see how we can refuse them any longer.'

Moody hesitated and then muttered, 'I'm not ready. I'm just not ready.'

'But were we ready in '73? Yet look how God blessed our ministry,' the singer responded.

'I must study more, Ira. I am finding it harder to prepare sermons now, so I must study the Word more. You see, I'm just not ready.' Moody's manner was earnest.

Sankey turned away from his friend and looked into the fire. Both men remained silent. After a few minutes Sankey looked back at Moody. 'D.L., you seem to have lost your fire. It was the Spirit that won souls five years ago not education,' he challenged.

His friend sat motionless in his big armchair and said nothing.

'Look, D.L.,' continued Sankey, 'why don't we go to England, and you can spend part of the time preaching and the rest studying. The opportunities for studying are greater there.'

'I can't,' grunted Moody.

Sankey could feel himself getting agitated at his friend's stubbornness. 'Why not?' he asked. His voice was unusually aggressive.

'I can't, Ira. Emma and I are expecting an addition to our family.'

Sankey's mouth fell open, and for a few moments he was lost for words. 'But why didn't you say that before? I didn't know.'

D.L. looked his friend in the eye. 'To be honest, Ira, I don't think it's the real reason why I won't go, but I guess it puts it out of the question for at least a year.'

Suddenly a big smile broke across Sankey's moustached face. 'Well, dear friend, my hearty congratulations. It's great news.' He stepped over to where Moody sat, stretched out his hand, and warmly clasped Moody's. 'Congratulations, D.L.'

Moody lifted his big frame from the chair and hugged his friend. He felt the tears trickling into his beard.

'D.L.,' said Sankey softly, 'I made a decision before I came here tonight, that if you wouldn't go with me I'd go alone.'

Moody stepped back. 'Go alone? What do you mean?'

'On a singing tour to England.'

A look of astonishment crossed Moody's face. 'But you can't go alone. I don't think it would work.'

'I don't see why not. The Lord blessed my singing when I toured with you; I don't believe he is incapable of doing so if I tour alone.'

Moody was not happy and he strongly urged his friend to reconsider. But it was clear that Sankey's mind was made up.

Before the end of the year Ira Sankey was on his way to England. His ministry failed.

Perhaps inspired by Sankey's enthusiasm, Moody went back into action. While the singer was in England, Moody took his family to Baltimore and began a series of meetings there. This campaign was quite deliberately different from most of those that had preceded it. This time no enormous halls were hired. Instead, the majority of the services were held in churches of varying denominations, and some in the Maryland Institute.

He was still committed heavily to study, and devoted the whole morning, six days a week, to it. He took meetings most afternoons and evenings, and usually preached four times on Sundays.

After the commencement of one of the services at the Maryland Institute a middle-aged man, with receding hair and greying moustache, entered the building. An usher offered him a hymnbook and tried to direct him to a vacant place.

'I won't be staying. I'm just looking for someone,' he gruffly replied. He began to walk slowly down the aisle looking intently at the faces in the congregation. At first Detective Todd Hall paid no attention to the large bewhiskered gentlemen speaking from a makeshift pulpit. He was more intent on finding the criminal whom he had seen enter the Institute a few minutes earlier. As he looked, Moody's words began to seep into his mind. Gradually thoughts of the criminal vanished and his attention became centred on the preacher.

Church-going was not his business, but Todd Hall found this man and his message fascinating.

' "And as Moses lifted up the serpent in the wilderness" ' he heard, ' "even so must the Son of Man be lifted up; that whosoever believeth in him should not perish but have everlasting life." '

Thoughts of his calling receded. He could hear a new call, the call of Jesus Christ. When the appeal was made at the end of the sermon, he was one of the first to respond, and become a Christian that evening. He knew that a dramatic change had been made in his life, and vowed to tell everyone about it. His first destination after the service was the City Hall, where he explained to his fellow detectives what had happened to him. 'Now boys,' he said, 'I am done with this life I have been living. I'm going to follow Jesus Christ. All I ask is don't ridicule me, but encourage me.'

The other policemen were astonished. This was not the Todd Hall they knew, but they put it down to a passing fad. 'He'll be alright in the morning,' they said.

From the City Hall he went home, where he fell on his knees in front of his wife. 'Annie,' he confessed, 'I left you this morning not worthy the name of a husband, not worthy the name of father to our children, but a little while ago at the Maryland Institute I determined to live a better life. Mr Moody told me what a sinner I was and that Jesus Christ wanted to save me, and he did.' He looked at his wife. 'Annie, kneel down with me and let us ask God to help me be a better man.'

Annie Hall was even more surprised than the detectives had been. Tears welled up in her eyes, and she knelt beside her husband. He prayed a short but fervent prayer, then they rose from their knees. She turned to her husband and said, 'Todd, if you have become a Christian then I want to be one too.' That night she gave her life to the Lord. Later, Todd Hall, became an evangelist.

Just before the end of Moody's Baltimore crusade, Emma gave birth to Paul Dwight Moody.

Moody and Sankey did not remain separated for too long. They campaigned together in St Louis during the following winter, 1879 – 80, and began talking about another trip to Britain. Invitations were still arriving, but it was not until September 1881 that they finally embarked for Liverpool.

Chapter 14

On arrival in England towards the end of 1881, Moody and Sankey began their work in Newcastle and then went on to Scotland. Though they met with considerable success, their impact was less than on their previous visit. The summer of 1882 saw them conduct a sequence of short campaigns throughout England and Wales.

Kynaston Studd, the eldest of the three Studd brothers, who were now all at Cambridge University, had contacted Moody early in 1882 suggesting that he hold a mission in Cambridge. Of the Studd brothers, he was the one who had grown most in the Christian life up to this time. He was president of the Cambridge Inter-Collegiate Christian Union. George had continued to run the Christian race quite well, but Charlie had put his cricket before his God and had played for England in the famous 'Ashes' Test. All three brothers were to captain the university cricket team in an age when it was a highly prestigious position.

Studd's invitation was one of many that Moody and Sankey received, and it was impossible for the evangelists to accept them all. In addition D.L. still felt his lack of education keenly, and was unusually wary about conducting a ministry in such a learned environment as Cambridge.

But the Holy Spirit gradually wore down Moody's reservations, and early in November they arrived at the university city.

The first meeting was held on Sunday, 5th November, at the Corn Exchange. Most of the 1,700 students who attended came out of curiosity and some had come with the simple intention of disrupting the service. Fireworks (it was Guy Fawkes day) were let off outside the building, and, within, Moody and Sankey were greeted with a mixture of boos and cheers. When Sankey sang, each verse was followed by calls of 'Hear! Hear!' from the trouble-makers. Moody's mode of speech was greeted with laughter, and the whole meeting just subsided into a farce.

The next day the ringleader in the mischief-makers called upon D.L. He was taken to Moody's room, and the evangelist greeted him with a warm shake of the hand. D.L. could feel the reluctance of the man's handshake.

'My name is Gerald Lander,' the visitor advised. 'I have come on behalf of the students to a . . . a . . . apologise.'

The American could detect the unwillingness in the Englishman's voice. He was clearly a pressed man rather than a volunteer.

He continued, 'I have a letter of apology for you, signed by some of the students.'

'Thank you, Mr Lander, thank you. Do sit down, won't you?' Moody indicated an armchair. The student hesitated for a moment then sat down.

'I do appreciate your apology, Mr Lander,' said the evangelist with a thoughtful look in his face. 'I wonder, Mr Lander, would you like to come to the series of meetings that we are holding in the Gymnasium in Market Passage this week? They are especially for the students of Cambridge University.'

Lander looked at Moody in blank amazement. He tried to speak, but the words wouldn't come.

'Bring your friends, too,' urged D.L.

'Well, I . . . I . . . I am rather b . . . b . . . busy at the moment,' stuttered the visitor in embarrassment.

'Nonsense!' claimed Moody. 'I'm sure you can find the time. Come and bring your friends.'

'No really, Mr er . . . Moody, I . . . I . . . I really don't think I can. If you will excuse me,' he said rising from his seat, 'I must be going.'

When Moody had said farewell to his visitor his grin

stretched from ear to ear.

On Wednesday afternoon Moody held a prayer meeting especially for the mothers of the university's students. Some 150 mothers attended.

That evening at the Gymnasium over 500 students were present to hear Moody and Sankey. At the appeal 52 came out and climbed the stairs to the inquiry room. One of them was Gerald Lander. Lander went on to become a missionary to China.

In December, George Studd fell ill – so ill that he was near to death. His brother Charlie spent hours at his bedside, and came under strong conviction about the order of his priorities. George's closeness to death had a profound influence upon him. When George began to recover, Charlie decided to seek out Moody and journeyed to Stratford to attend the evangelist's meetings. It was there that he experienced a fresh encounter with God and from then he burned with zeal to spread the Gospel.

Within a few weeks Charlie Studd was a major influence in the conversion of Wilfred Grenfell, who was later to become a missionary to Labrador.

Just over two years later C.T. Studd was to leave England as a missionary bound for China. God had become number one in his life. Along with him were six other Cambridge men, and they became known as the Cambridge Seven. All of them had been either converted through the ministry of Moody and Sankey or strongly influenced by them. Studd was later to become founder of the Worldwide Evangelisation Crusade.

After Moody arrived back in America he came to recognise the value of another aspect of his work. Though he himself was not called to the missionfields of Asia or Africa, he realised that he was a means of inspiring others to answer such a call. The example of the Cambridge Seven was planted firmly in his mind.

Back in 1880 he had arranged a Bible Conference at Northfield where various speakers from America and

Britain expounded the Word. The event was repeated the following year. The third such conference was held in August 1885. One of the speakers was Kynaston Studd, and the conference took on a strong world mission emphasis. A full day was given over to prayer for missions and a small committee was set up to write 'An Appeal to Disciples Everywhere', which was a plea for increased missionary endeavour.

That year Moody began to preach at some of the great American universities including Princeton and Yale. He had now overcome his feeling of inferiority in the presence of the intellectual, recognising that the Holy Spirit could apply his humble words to the most intelligent of doubters.

In 1886, with the help of a YMCA leader, L.T. Wishard, he called the first Christian Student Conference. This was held at the Mt Hermon Boys' School. From this conference the Student Volunteers movement emerged.

The Student Volunteers had four aims: 'First, to awaken and foster among all the Christian students of the United States and Canada, intelligent and active interest in foreign missions. Second, to enrol a sufficient number of properly qualified student volunteers to meet the successive demands of the various missionary Boards of North America. Third, to help all such as pledge themselves to foreign missionary work to prepare for their life work. Fourth, to lay an equal burden of responsibility on all students who are to remain as ministers and lay workers at home, that they may actively promote missionary enterprise by intelligent advocacy, gifts and prayers.'

Moody saw clearly the importance of missionary work, and realised that the church had a responsibility to send the best people available.

In 1887 no less than 400 attended the second Christian Student Conference, and the Student Volunteers rapidly gained in influence.

There are two types of people who value quality

education; those who lacked it and regret that, and those who experienced it and are grateful for it. Moody was clearly in the former category. He had founded the two schools in Northfield, and been a major influence in establishing the Student Volunteers. But a further educational endeavour was yet to come.

He had been increasingly concerned during his campaigns about the absence of suitable people to counsel inquirers. He and Sankey usually did the task with the help of a handful of ministers. But the inquirers nearly always outnumbered those able to aid them. What was needed, he believed, was an institute to train Christian workers for this and other tasks.

Early in 1886 he had set about raising funds for the project, and in 1887 with John Farwell and a few other friends he formed the Chicago Evangelisation Society. The purpose of this society was to build and run a Bible Institute. A series of obstacles hindered the plan, and at one stage Moody resigned from the society, but later rejoined it. It was not until 26th September, 1889, that the Bible Institute of the Chicago Evangelisation Society (later to be renamed Moody Bible Institute) was opened.

Eighty students were enrolled initially, and the number increased rapidly, rising to about 300 within a few years.

Though the programme of the institute was largely academic, every student had to engage in practical ministry. Neither Moody nor R.A. Torrey, its principal, could see Christianity as a purely intellectual pursuit. Lectures on the Bible and its theology were joined by mission work in slums, ministry among children and evangelistic crusades. The Bible Institute quickly became an influential force in Christian circles.

Chapter 15

In the autumn of 1891 Moody and Sankey began their last visit to Britain together, though Sankey was to make one further visit on his own. They had received an invitation from Scotland in the form of a scroll containing 2,000 signatures, and after initial hesitation had agreed to accept it. During the winter they held meetings in nearly 100 different towns and were warmly received wherever they went. To their delight they discovered that many people converted in their earlier campaigns were active in the churches. They also found that a high percentage of the younger ministers in the Scottish churches they visited had come to Christ during their previous visits.

None knew that this would be the duo's last time in Scotland, but some may have suspected it. Moody was now an enormous figure, greatly overweight, and looking older than his fifty-four years. Though he claimed good health he was beginning to slow down. Holidays for Moody had been a rarity all his life. Though he had always tried to observe a weekly Sabbath rest on any convenient day, usually Saturday, he was essentially a man of action, and holidays did not appeal to him.

But in the spring of 1892 one of his Scottish friends, Peter McKinnon, invited D.L. and his family to accompany him on a trip to Rome and the Holy Land. The invitation was accepted and D.L., his wife and youngest son, Paul, joined McKinnon and his wife on the holiday. Though holiday it was, the evangelist missed no opportunity to preach and conducted services in Rome, Jerusalem, Cairo and, on the way back to England, Naples and Paris. One one occasion he incited the anger of the Muslims by inadvertently preaching in one of their graveyards.

He was disappointed with many of the sacred sites, but found great delight in walking on the Mount of Olives, 'in his Master's footsteps'. Nearby Bethany, too, was a place of great fascination for him.

Back in Britain he preached throughout the summer and into autumn. In September he spoke at the Metropolitan Tabernacle in London, where C.H. Spurgeon (who had died that year) had been the minister. Moody's wife, daughter and youngest son returned to America in August and Will was studying in Germany. So for the last part of his work in Britain he soldiered on without the support of his family.

He booked his return passage to America in the German liner *Spree*, and Will decided to join him. But before he left England, Moody agreed to see a heart specialist, Sir Andrew Clark. In spite of his protestations to the contrary, his health was showing signs of decline.

Clark was most concerned about Moody's condition and asked about his workload. 'How often do you preach, Mr Moody?'

'Three times a day, usually, doctor. But on Sundays four or even five,' came the reply.

'And how many days a week?'

'Six normally, but seven lately,' confessed Moody.

'You're a fool, sir, a fool! You're killing yourself!' accused Sir Andrew.

Moody was not used to being called a fool, at least not in a doctor's surgery. 'Well, I do usually rest on Saturday, but it has been difficult to do so this year,' he protested. Moody thought for a moment, and then asked, 'And how many hours a day do you work, Sir Andrew?'

Now it was the doctor's turn to be surprised. 'Oh! I suppose about sixteen or seventeen.'

'And how many days a week?'

'Seven,' came the answer.

'Then you're a bigger fool than I am!' burst forth the evangelist. 'You'll kill yourself first.'

The doctor's visit concluded with Clark advising Moody to slow down. His heart could not stand the exhausting pace that he had set himself. Within a year Clark himself had died.

Moody and his son embarked upon the *Spree* on 23rd November. D.L. was still uncomfortable about sea travel, and for the first three days he spent most of the time in his bunk feeling sorry for himself. He had been considering Sir Andrew's warning and debating whether he should heed it or not. Soon after his return to America, he was due to participate in a massive campaign designed to coincide with the World's Fair being held in Chicago in 1893. The workload would be considerable, and he was thinking of ways to reduce the burden without it being detrimental to that vital series of meetings.

He had almost convinced himself that he should take a quieter role when there was a tremendous crash and the whole ship shuddered. D.L. sat upright. After a moment's hesitation, Will ran from the cabin and hurried to the deck.

A few minutes later Will returned with terrible news. 'Father, the shaft has broken, and . . . I think we're sinking.'

D.L. dressed quickly and father and son hurried up to the deck. The deck teemed with passengers all anxiously trying to establish the seriousness of the situation. The stern of the vessel was already clearly lower in the water than the bow. Captain Willigerod urged the passengers to return to their cabins, insisting that there was no immediate danger. Most heeded the captain's instruction, but some found their cabins inundated with quickly rising water, and hastily returned to the deck shouting the frightening news.

The pumps were working overtime, but the water level continued to rise. The seas were heavy and the *Spree* seemed in a helpless predicament. The captain and his officers considered the frightening choice of remaining on the floundering ship or lowering the lifeboats in the rough sea.

By noon the water level had ceased to rise. Though the *Spree* still drifted helplessly, the immediate danger was over. The stern now was even lower in the water and the bow correspondingly higher. There was nothing they could do except send up flares and wait for another vessel to spot them.

The following night Moody described as 'the darkest in all our lives. Seven hundred men, women and children waited for the doom that was settling upon us. We were all together in the saloon – Jews, Protestants, Catholics and sceptics – although I doubt if at that time there were any sceptics among us.'

Moody's feelings amid the crisis were understandably mixed. 'There was no cloud between my soul and my Saviour,' he wrote later. 'I knew my sins had been put away and that if I died there it would be only to wake up in heaven. But as my thoughts went out to my loved ones at home I realised that perhaps the next hour would separate me forever from them, so far as this world was concerned. I confess it almost broke me down. It was the darkest hour of my life!' But as the vessel continued to toss about in the sea, and he prayed to his God, a sweet peace came into his heart. Let it be Northfield or heaven, it made no difference now, he thought.

The next day, Sunday, Moody held a service in the main saloon. He read Psalm 91 and led the people in prayer, asking God for deliverance.

They went to bed that night with still no prospect of rescue, but D.L. slept soundly. At three a.m. he was woken up by the excited voice of his son. 'It's a ship, father. Come and see.' Father and son rushed up to the deck. As Moody looked in the direction of his son's pointing finger he could see a light rising and sinking in the swelling sea.

The *Lake Huron*, a freighter bound for Liverpool, had seen the flares and steamed to the rescue. It was able to tow the *Spree* back to Ireland, a distance of a thousand miles.

Long before D.L. disembarked in Ireland he had decided not to ease up. He was determined now to carry on with the World's Fair campaign with all the energy he could muster. His heart would stand the strain for as long as God needed him in this world. A verse from Psalm 91 kept coming back to him with a whole new meaning: 'For he shall give his angels charge over thee, to keep thee in all thy ways.'

Dwight L. Moody never suffered from seasickness again.

Chapter 16

Moody sailed for America on the next available vessel, the *Eturia*, and arrived home by mid-December. His mind now was filled with thoughts of the World's Fair and how best to make an impact for Christ during it.

The first service was held at the end of May and the last at the end of October. During that period nearly two million people attended the services led by Moody and Sankey and other evangelists. The attendance figures were kept by members of the Bible Institute. Moody himself was contemptuous of statistics. Once when asked if he kept records of the number of converts at his meetings, he responded, 'Records! Records! They are only kept in heaven.' If he did not consider records important, the stories of lives dramatically changed by the grace of God were vital to him. The fair attracted people from all over America, and from many other parts of the world, and many of those visitors came face to face with the gospel message proclaimed by Moody and his associates.

The meetings were held at strategic centres throughout the city in churches, including the Chicago Avenue Church, theatres and any suitable public building.

At one service in a circus tent D.L. preached on the verse: 'The Son of Man is come to seek and to save that which was lost.' During his sermon a living illustration appeared before him, a crying child walking slowly between the preacher and the crowd, having been lost in the dense throng. Moody, never one to fail to see what was going on in even the most crowded auditorium, interrupted his sermon and stepped down from the platform. He picked up the child and mounted the platform again with the little boy in his arms. As the preacher looked out at the crowd before him, a figure, the boy's father, moved from his seat and quickly joined Moody on the stage. As he handed the child back to his father, tears filled the evangelist's eyes. He addressed the congregation again. 'You see this is what Jesus Christ came to do; he came to seek and save sinners, and to restore them to their heavenly Father's embrace.' The people were deeply moved by the enacted parable, and many responded at the end of the service.

The campaign had a great impact on Chicago and beyond, and spawned new movements and caused others to grow rapidly. Such was its influence on society that the press began to speak of the 'new puritanism', as Christians made their presence felt in many areas of public life.

Dwight L. Moody had been true to his vow made on the *Spree*. And God Almighty anointed him with the power that only he can give.

Sankey had missed out on the trip to the Holy Land in 1892, but he had his opportunity to travel there and to Egypt six years later. As Moody had been called upon to preach during his visit, the frequently recognised Sankey was also asked to sing. On one occasion in Cairo when he had declined because there was no instrument present, a lady left the hall accompanied by four Egyptian soldiers. They returned a few minutes later with a small organ, and Sankey sang to the small company of Britons, Americans and Egyptians.

Chapter 17

In 1894 there was great rejoicing in the Moody household. In May the young Emma was married to Percy Fitt (D.L.'s secretary), and Will married Major Whittle's daughter, May, in August. The following year saw the birth of Irene Moody in August and Emma Fitt just before Christmas. D.L. was delighted. He had always had a great love for children, but it was never better expressed than in his tenderness towards his grandchildren.

He used to write letters to them full of gentleness and fun. When she was a mere three weeks old Emma received a letter from her doting grandfather.

It read: 'This is my first letter to you my dear little grandchild. I wanted to get a letter to you before you got your first tooth. Hurry up and get them before the hot weather comes, for I will get you some candy, and you will want teeth to eat it. I want you to hurry up and grow, so I can come early mornings and take you out riding when your father and mother are fast asleep. We will slip off over the river to see Irene and have some good times.'

The mid and later 1890s were a strange mixture of happiness and tragedy in the life of the ageing evangelist. In February 1896 his mother died. He had always been very close to her, and though he rejoiced in her going to heaven, he felt her loss keenly. Another grandchild, Dwight Lyman Moody Jnr., was born in November 1897.

He loved to ride through the streets of Northfield in his buggy with his grandchildren by his side. On one occasion when he was riding with little Irene, she fell asleep leaning on him. When he pulled up at his house, rather than wake the child, he asked someone else to unharness the horse, and just sat there motionless with the child blissfully resting beside him. The day was warm, and it wasn't long before he fell asleep too.

But Dwight Moody still laboured on, and towards the end of 1898 he went west to campaign in Colorado, Arizona and California. Sankey was not with him on this trip, as he had not enjoyed the best of health since his return from the Holy Land. Instead, D.L. was accompanied by another singer, D.B. Towner.

While in Colorado, Moody received a telegram with some shattering news. On 30th November, his one-year-old grandson Dwight had died. Moody was distressed.

But he wrote to the grieving parents: 'How I wish I could be with you to comfort you, but the Lord will comfort you. I know Dwight has gone to help get things ready for his parents. He was the last to come into our circle, and he is the first to go up there! I do thank God for such a life. It was nearly all smiles and sunshine. I cannot think of him as belonging to earth. The more I think of him the more I think he was only sent to us to draw us all closer to each other and up to the world of light and joy. Thank God, Dwight is safe at home, and we will all of us see him soon.'

Moody continued proclaiming Christ in the west, but with a heavy heart, and in March he received news that Irene had pneumonia. For days he fretted and prayed and eventually received news from Will that the little girl was improving. Though he had been told that Irene was still a sick child he felt relieved.

While on this tour he received an invitation to tour Australia and New Zealand, but such were the calls on his time that he replied that he was unable to accept it.

Upon his return to Northfield he discovered that Irene now had tuberculosis. He invited Will and his family to move in with him, which they did. To see his grandaughter so desperately sick upset him terribly. He spent a lot of time with her, neglecting to reply to letters (writing never was his strong point) and frequently absenting himself from meetings at the Northfield conference.

One of the speakers at the conference was F.B. Meyer, and when he showed the Englishman Irene's pet lamb, Moody broke down and sobbed convulsively. Meyer could feel the tears pouring down his own cheeks as he moved to comfort his friend.

On 22nd August she died. Moody was downcast. The funeral was held in the open air. Moody, looking older than his sixty-two years, came forward to address the mourners. For a few moments it seemed as though he would be unable to speak as he struggled with his emotions. Then quietly and slowly he poured out his heart.

'I have been thinking this morning about the aged prophet waiting in the valley of the Jordan, so many years ago, for the chariot of God to take him home.' He paused for what seemed an age. Sobs could be heard from various sections of the gathering. 'The chariot of God came down to the Connecticut valley yesterday morning and took our little Irene home. The one was taken at the end of years of active service; the other at the early dawn of youth. But the service of the prophet was no more complete than that of the little handmaid of the Lord, for God called both, and he never interrupts the service of his own.

'Irene has finished her course. Her work was well wrought on earth. She has accomplished more than many in their three score years and ten. We would not have her back, although her voice was the sweetest I have ever heard on earth. She never met me once since she was three months old, until the last few days of pain, without a smile. But Christ has some service for her above'.

He wiped the tears from his eyes before proceeding. 'I thank God this morning for the hope of immortality. I know I shall see her in the morning, more beautiful in her resurrection glory than she was here.'

Chapter 18

Though Moody still felt the loss of his granddaughter very deeply, there was never any question of withdrawing into himself. There was still work to do, still Christ to proclaim. On 8th November he left Northfield bound for Kansas City where he was due to conduct a week-long campaign. The meetings were to be held in the gigantic Convention Hall, which had been built out of public subscriptions. Its seating capacity was 15,000.

The first service was held on Sunday afternoon, and the great hall was packed. An interdenominational choir of 500 was assembled, which sang, as Moody described it, 'famously well'. He joked that at first the choirmaster had had problems because the Methodists sang quickly and the Presbyterians at a slower pace. 'But we have taught them to pull together pretty well now,' he said with a laugh.

Everything seemed fine. The people came in their thousands. Moody preached with power and many were converted to the Lord Jesus. But something was wrong. Moody was a very sick man. He preached twice daily that week, but after the Wednesday evening service he was so exhausted he excused himself from attending the inquirers' meeting. At the afternoon meeting the following day he repeatedly had to lean on the pulpit to support himself.

On the Thursday evening, though he was finding walking difficult, he preached again. Standing unsteadily he began: 'We read in the fourteenth chapter of Luke, verses 16 to 18, these words. ''A certain man made a great supper, and bade many; and sent his servant at supper time to say them that were bidden, 'Come; for all things are now ready.' And they all with one consent began to make excuse''.' He was on one of his favourite themes, the excuses of men.

As he warmed to his task his strength seemed to increase. He spoke of the excuses given by the men in our Lord's parable. He likened them to the excuses that modern man made to avoid following Jesus. And as he drew his message to a close he said: 'Suppose we shoud write out tonight this excuse, how would it sound? "To the King of Heaven: While sitting in Convention Hall, Kansas City, on November 16, 1899, I received a very pressing invitation from one of your servants to be present at the marriage supper of your only begotten Son".'

He paused for a moment, and then said in a mock arrogant tone: ' "I pray thee have me excused." '

Again he paused. The crowd was hushed.

'Would you sign that, young man?' he challenged. 'Would you, mother? Would you come up to the reporter's table, take a pen and put your name down to such an excuse? I doubt if there is one here, who would sign it.'

'Will you, then, pay no attention to God's invitation? I beg of you do not make light of it. It is a loving God inviting you to a feast, and God is not mocked. Go play with forked lightning, but trifle not with God.'

'Just let me write out another answer. "To the King of Heaven: While sitting in Convention Hall, Kansas City, on November 16, 1899, I received a pressing invitation from one of your messengers to be present at the marriage supper of your only begotten Son. I hasten to reply. By the grace of God I will be present." '

'Who will sign that?' he called out. 'Is there one here who will put his name to that? Is there one who will say, "By the grace of God I will accept the invitation now"? May God bring you to a decision now.'

The inquiry rooms were full that night, but Moody was too tired to be present. The next day he was so sick he was unable to preach. Dr Schauffler examined him and insisted that he should not participate any further in the meetings in Kansas City because his heart would not stand it. He urged him to go home to rest. D.L. looked at the doctor. 'Doctor, it is more painful to me to give up those audiences, than it is to suffer from my ailments, but I know you are right.'

He left Kansas City on the Friday and arrived back in Northfield on Sunday. Though he was obviously very unwell, no one was greatly alarmed at his condition. Moody himself was optimistic. He was looking forward to preaching again. But his condition gradually deteriorated and by 21st December he was very weak, and concern for him greatly increased.

The following day, after a restless night, his son Will heard him say, 'Earth is receding; heaven is opening before me. This is no dream. It is beautiful. If this is death it is sweet. God is calling me and I must go. Don't call me back.'

His wife had been resting, but she was immediately called back to her husband's bedside. She knelt beside him and held his hand. Again he spoke.

'Mama,' he whispered, 'you have been a good dear wife.' He then slid into unconsciousness. Later he was heard to say, 'Is this dying? Why, this is bliss,' and later still, 'There is no valley'.

He regained consciousness and hope flickered again. 'If God wished he could work a miracle,' he said. He struggled to get up and insisted that they let him sit in his chair, which they did, but soon he returned to his bed. It was as if the final exertion of that movement was the last straw for the lion's heart of D.L. Moody; he died almost straight away. Dwight Lyman Moody had gone to be with his Lord.

His funeral was attended by a most varied congregation. Many noted figures from the evangelical churches were present, including Dr C.I. Scofield, Wilbur Chapman and Dr R.A. Torrey. Leaders from the business world, students from Northfield and Mt Hermon Schools, and the people from Northfield and the surrounding districts filled the church. Included among the mourners was Ira

David Sankey. Apart from the immediate family, perhaps he felt the loss most of all.

Early in the New Year a memorial service was held for Moody. One of the speakers, Dr A.C. Dixon, paid him the tribute of tributes, when he said, 'There was no need that D.L. Moody should ever perform a miracle. He was a Miracle.'

Sankey tried to continue where his friend had left off, conducting evangelistic services in America and both singing and preaching. In August 1900 he made his final visit to Britain, spending an exhausting two months travelling and preaching throughout the British Isles.

On his return to America he settled in Brooklyn and joined Lafayette Avenue Presbyterian Church. He was invited by a Christian newspaper to conduct a song service in the Tombs Prison in New York. It was a daunting experience. The prisoners were not allowed to leave their cells for the service, but Sankey and his companions proceeded with the service in a central part of the prison. His voice was not as strong as in his younger days, nor the tone so fine, but he was heard by many of the gaol's inmates as he sang 'Jesus, Lover of my Soul' and 'The Ninety and Nine'.

In 1902, age and weariness forced him to give up the work to which he had dedicated his life, and he returned to a quiet life with rarely a public appearance. But for a while he still continued working on a new hymbook.

As far back as 1893 he had begun to have trouble with his eyesight, but now he began to experience further deterioration in his vision and considerable pain in his eyes. His physician diagnosed glaucoma. Within six months he was totally blind.

His final years were filled with sickness, and his wife and family watched him slip slowly and agonisingly from them. At times he seemed cheerful in spite of his infirmities; at others he was very low.

During the summer of 1908 he was visited by Dr A.C. Dixon,

who found him a shadow of his former self. He was lying in bed barely moving.

'How are you, Brother Sankey?' asked Dixon.

'I think you might have to speak louder, doctor, I'm afraid his hearing is not too good now.' It was one of Sankey's sons, Allan.

Dixon enquired again.

Sankey heard that time, and his face responded as he recognised the voice. He struggled to speak. 'Near the throne,' he muttered. 'Near the throne.'

Dixon gave greetings to him from his friends in Chicago. A smile lit up the singer's face. 'What a meeting, what a meeting that will be!' came the hoarse response.

Dixon could feel tears welling up in his eyes. 'I sometimes think of Mr Moody in heaven', he said. 'I am sure he's still working up there.'

'Yes,' said Sankey, 'I can still hear him say, "Come on, Sankey, don't let's be late for the meeting".'

A few weeks later, on 13th August, Ira David Sankey died in his sleep. But his spirit sings on:

There's a land that is fairer than day,
    And by faith we can see it afar,
For the Father awaits o'er the way,
    To prepare us a dwelling place there.

We shall sing on that beautiful shore
    The melodious songs of the blessed,
And our spirits shall sorrow no more –
    Not a sigh for the blessing of rest.

In the sweet by-and-by
    We shall meet on that beautiful shore.
In the sweet by-and-by
    We shall meet on that beautiful shore.

Bibliography

Wilbur Chapman   *The Life and Work of D.L. Moody*, James Nisbet, London, 1900.

W.H. Daniels,   *D.L. Moody and his Work*, Hodder & Stoughton, London, 1875.

A.P. Fitt,   *The Life of D.L. Moody*, Moody Press, Chicago.

J.C. Pollock,   *Moody Without Sankey*, Hodder & Stoughton, London, 1963.

I.D. Sankey,   *My Life and the Story of the Gospel Hymns*, Harper Brothers, New York, 1906.